Music Theory Translation Series

CLAUDE V. PALISCA, EDITOR

Musica Enchiriadis and Scolica Enchiriadis

TRANSLATED, WITH
INTRODUCTION AND
NOTES, BY RAYMOND
ERICKSON • EDITED BY
CLAUDE V. PALISCA

Yale University Press
New Haven & London

The preparation of this work was made possible in part by a grant from the National Endowment for the Humanities, an independent federal agency.

Printed in the United States of America.

Library of Congress Cataloging-in-Publication Data
Musica enchiriadis. English
    Musica enchiriadis ; and, Scolica enchiriadis / translated, with introduction and notes, by Raymond Erickson ; edited by Claude V. Palisca.
    p.   cm. — (Music theory translation series)
Includes bibliographical references (p.   ) and index.
ISBN 0-300-05818-7
1. Music—Theory—500–1400—Early works to 1800.   I. Erickson, Raymond.   II. Palisca, Claude V.   III. Scolica enchiriadis. English.   IV. Title.   V. Title: Scolica enchiriadis.   VI. Series.
MT5.5.M8713   1995
781'.09'02—dc20
'94-34601
CIP
MN

A catalogue record for this book is available from the British Library.
The paper in this book meets the guidelines for permanence and durability of the Committee on Production Guidelines for Book Longevity of the Council on Library Resources.

10   9   8   7   6   5   4   3   2   1

For Carole

Contents

Foreword by the Series Editor

The two treatises that share the puzzling term *enchiriadis,* which is poor Greek and worse Latin, are famous most of all for their discussion and illustration of the earliest written polyphony and the graphic representation of melody in the daseian notation. The examples in which the voices sing in parallel fourths, fifths, and octaves struck the earliest readers of the treatises as exotic in their primitive ignorance of the most inviolable rule of strict counterpoint, the prohibition of parallel perfect consonances. But this is how counterpoint began. A patient integral reading of the two treatises is rewarded by the revelation of much more: a rich world of musical thought that lets us penetrate the minds of ninth-century musicians and teachers. It is this kind of reading that the Music Theory Translation Series has aimed to stimulate.

The *Enchiriadis* tracts are the most important body of medieval music theory that has lacked adequate translation into a modern language. Apparently written in the second half of the ninth century, the two anonymous treatises are approximately contemporary with Hucbald's *De harmonica institutione,* which is translated by Warren Babb in one of the first volumes of our series, *Hucbald, Guido, and John on Music* (1978). In their pedagogic goals, the *Enchiriadis* treatises stand somewhere between Hucbald's work and Guido's in that they orient the reader in the current practice of plainchant and organum while building on the theoretical foundation of Greek theory as transmitted by Boethius in his *De institutione musica* (translated in our series as *Fundamentals of Music* by Calvin M. Bower, 1989). *Musica enchiriadis* was the one treatise besides Boethius's that Guido named in his writings, though he thought it was by a certain Odo. Thus the present volume very much belongs in the core of the documents necessary for the study of early music theory translated in our series.

The two treatises are not glosses upon previous texts but are original in content and form, though, of course, dependent on previous writings. The use of fixed-pitch notation and of chants written in such a notation rather than cited by their text incipits, the unambiguous description of singing in parts, and the technical discussion of melody in terms of the finals and ranges of the plainchant modes—these are some of the pioneering steps these two anonymous authors took. They also made a major breakthrough in that they justified departing from purely parallel part-singing, which must have already been common in the heterophony of popular and folk music. It is this independence of vocal lines that launched European music in a direction that distinguished it from that of other peoples.

More than other treatises published in this series, the *Enchiriadis* tracts demand both the guidance of an extended introduction and copious annotations. Raymond Erickson's transparent and fluent translation is apt to make us overlook the complications, implications, and mysteries revealed in the footnotes. Erickson's is the first translation to take advantage of the critical edition by Hans Schmid published in 1981 by the Bavarian Academy of Sciences in Munich, to which we are greatly indebted for permission to base our translation on Schmid's Latin text. Erickson dedicated intensive study to the terminology of the period at the centers for musical terminology at that Academy and at the Albert-Ludwig University in Freiburg. This translation has been the focus of his research for more than ten years, though he was often distracted by other projects, such as building the faculty of what is now the Aaron Copland School of Music at Queens College of the City University of New York and organizing a series of interdisciplinary summer institutes, or "academies," through the Aston Magna Foundation and the National Endowment for the Humanities.

A grant from the Translations Program of the NEH provided support for the preparation of this book.

CLAUDE V. PALISCA

Translator's Acknowledgments

But as I now write this down, I am already beginning to notice how difficult it is . . . to choose just the right words—and how much ambiguity, how much misunderstanding, is inherent in the simplest utterance.—*Stefan Zweig*, Phantastische Nacht

---

The completion of this volume has taken much longer than expected, the result of frequent interruptions caused by other professional obligations. Nonetheless, it is my feeling that the final product is the better for having had such a long gestation period, even though there are also attendant risks. A translation is perforce an interpretation, but I have tried to achieve objectivity and accuracy by studying, as far as conditions permitted, the histories and uses of terms employed in the *Musica enchiriadis* and *Scolica enchiriadis* up through the ninth century and also by comparing the sometimes different uses of words by the authors of the two treatises. This approach, plus the use of Hans Schmid's critical edition of the *Enchiriadis* treatises, which was not available to previous translators, distinguishes this effort from earlier translations by Leonie Rosenstiel and Richard Holladay.

Originally I prepared extensive annotations to the translation summarizing the terminological studies, but it was felt that, in keeping with the format of this series, such information should be published elsewhere. One study by the translator, dealing with a small group of terms, is listed in the bibliography.

To what degree I have attained my objectives of accuracy and comprehensibility will be judged by others. But there is no question that many people and institutions have assisted me in the quest of them. A first word of thanks goes to Claude V. Palisca, who assigned me, as a first-year graduate student many years ago, the task of translating a portion of *Musica enchiriadis* and in 1979 invited me to undertake the present translation for the Yale Music Theory Translation Series. In the intervening years I have come to appreciate even more than before his Solomonic wisdom as editor and scholar, not to mention his Job-like patience.

A fellowship from the Alexander von Humboldt Stiftung made possible periods of research at the musicological seminar of the Albert-Ludwig University in Freiburg and the Bavarian Academy of Sciences in Munich, both important centers of terminological studies. In Freiburg, under the sponsorship of Hans Heinrich Eggebrecht, I worked closely with Fritz Reckow and visited a seminar on the *Musica enchiriadis* given by Professor Eggebrecht, founder of the *Handwörterbuch der musikalischen Terminologie,* that rekindled my interest in the treatise. In Munich, under the sponsorship of Theodor Göllner, I benefited from the daily contact with Michael Bernhard, editor of the *Lexicon musicum latinum,* and also had available to me the unique source materials of the *Thesaurus linguae latinae* (under Peter Flury) and the *Mittellateinishes Wörterbuch* (under Theresia Payr). At home in New York, I had available the fine music library of the Aaron Copland School of Music at Queens College (headed by Joseph Ponte, ever alert for new materials of interest to me), and also drew on the rich resources of the New York Public Library and the libraries of Union Theological Seminary and Columbia University. I am also very grateful to Calvin Bower for sending me a prepublication typescript of his translation of Boethius's *De institutione musica.*

Along the way, various individuals have read drafts of portions of this volume, and have made suggestions that I have willingly adopted. Nancy Phillips, whose New York University dissertation is a landmark in the study of the *Enchiriadis* treatises, early on gave important corrective advice and generously offered assistance. Although I have come to different conclusions about the interpretation of some terms in the treatises, her work caused me to think about many of these problems in the first place and I gratefully acknowledge my indebtedness to her. Prof. Robert Newman, now a classicist at the University of Hawaii, took considerable time to read carefully rough draft translations of both treatises while he was an NEH Fellow working on the *Thesaurus linguae latinae.* Fritz Reckow, Claude V. Palisca, and I have used draft versions, open to student comment, in courses at Ohio State University, Yale University, and the Graduate School of the City University of New York (where I credit in particular the sharp eye of Mark Anson-Cartwright). Charles Atkinson has been generous with both his friendship and advice, having read the introduction and part of the translations. Brien Weiner, when an undergraduate at Queens College, worked with me closely for over a year as a tutee and research assistant, discovering in the process many infelicities in the translations as well as typographical and other errors. Subsequently, Halina Goldberg read the final draft version and Emerson Chen was of great assistance in the computer generation of the musical examples. Also thanks to Grace Romeo of the Queens College Word Processing department for the remarkably accurate typing of the Latin text of both treatises in a form I found very useful for the initial stages of this work. Last, but certainly not least, I wish to thank Harry Haskell, music editor of Yale University Press, for his commitment to this book and for the support and cooperation he has given me while gently shepherding the volume through the final editing and production stages.

There are personal as well as professional debts to acknowledge. In Germany, my work was encouraged and stimulated by the hospitality offered by Fritz and Elke Reckow, Wolfgang and Edith Ruf, and the Dietmar Dagefoerde family in Freiburg, and by Evelyn Aschenbach, Horst Rek, and Gudrun Schiller in Munich. But the biggest debt of all I owe to Carole De-Saram, who married not only me but also an uncompleted book that necessitated several periods of separation, patiently endured, before the work was completed. It is to her that this volume is rightfully and lovingly dedicated.

Abbreviations

HdMT   Hans Heinrich Eggebrecht, ed. *Handwörterbuch der musika-lischen Terminologie*. Wiesbaden: Franz Steiner, 1972–.

PL   Jacques-Paul Migne, ed. *Patrologiae cursus completus, series latina*. Paris: Brepols, 1844–86.

Introduction

The treatises known commonly today as *Musica enchiriadis* [ME] and *Scolica enchiriadis* [SE] are products of ninth-century reverence for and interest in the received wisdom of antiquity.[1] But even more they reflect concern for the training and education of singers engaged in daily worship.[2] Indeed, the pragmatic stance of these documents, evident in the inclusion of exercises and of music from the repertory—features totally absent from the ancient formal treatments of music—testifies to Carolingian practicality. This introduction will survey the contents of the two treatises and their relation to each other; their sources of inspiration, authority, and vocabulary; and some resonances of the treatises in post-Carolingian times.

---

1. The Latin text used for the translations is the modern critical edition of the treatises by Hans Schmid, *Musica et scolica enchiriadis una cum aliquibus tractatulis adiunctis* (Munich: Verlag der Bayerischen Akademie der Wissenschaften, 1981). References to specific passages in that edition will be made by page and line number in forms such as "3.5–8" (page 3, lines 5 through 8), "14.5,8" (page 14, lines 5 and 8), and 93.*descriptio* 3 (page 93, *descriptio* 3). In cases of possible ambiguity, the page number will be preceded by "Schmid." In Schmid's edition *Musica enchiriadis* occupies pp. 3–59, *Scolica enchiriadis* pp. 60–156.

2. SE specifically addresses itself to the needs of the *peritus cantor*, the skilled and informed singer; cf. 60f.10f.

ORIGINS

The Literary Sources

The two treatises quote or paraphrase (usually without attribution) many Latin writings on music that had come down to the ninth century; in fact, the breadth and sometimes clever use of these borrowings is unmatched in the medieval music-theoretic literature. The principal late classical sources represented, in approximate chronological order, are:

> Censorinus, *De die natali* (A.D. 238)
> Calcidius, translation and commentary on Plato's *Timaeus* (4th century)
> Augustine, *De musica* (A.D. 387–9)
> Fulgentius, *Mitologiae* (5th–6th centuries)
> Boethius, *De institutione arithmetica* and *De institutione musica* (before 510)
> Cassiodorus, *Institutiones* (540)[3]

The *Enchiriadis* treatises also draw on Vergil's *Aeneid,* the Vulgate (Paul's Epistle to the Romans), Augustine's *De ordine,* and Boethius's *Consolatio philosophiae.*[4]

Notably absent from these lists is Martianus Capella's *De nuptiis Philologiae et Mercurii,* the most popular treatment of the liberal arts. Vitruvius's *De architectura,* Quintilian's *Institutio oratoria,* Macrobius's *Commentarium in somnium Scipionis,* Favonius Eulogius's *Disputatio de somnio Scipionis,* and Isidore of Seville's *Etymologiae* also contain discussions of music that are not directly quoted.

Despite their incorporation of received ideas, the *Enchiriadis* treatises are highly innovative. In them are found for the first time—if one accepts a

---

3. The principal passages drawing on these sources are as follows: Censorinus, *De die natali liber,* ed. Nicolaus Sallmann (Leipzig: Teubner, 1983), 10.4–6 (Sallmann, p. 16); Schmid 23.1–7. Calcidius, *Timaeus a Calcidius translatus commentarioque instructus,* ed. Jan Hendrik Waszink (London: Warburg Institute, 1962), 1.44 (p. 92); Schmid 3.1–7. Augustine, *De musica,* ed. Giovanni Marzi (Florence: G. C. Sansoni, 1969), 1:2,2 (p. 86); Schmid 60.1. The section on rhythm beginning Schmid 86.384 also owes much to this work despite the absence of direct quotations. Fulgentius, *Opera,* ed. Rudolf Helm (Stuttgart: Teubner, 1970), 3.10 (pp. 77f.); Schmid 57.1ff. Boethius, *De institutione arithmetica,* ed. Gottfried Friedlein (Leipzig, 1857; repr. Frankfurt a. M.: Minerva, 1966), 1.1 (Schmid 107.165–8; 108.185–90); 1.21 (Schmid 118.42–8); 1.22 (Schmid 118f.52–8); 1.24 (Schmid 120.73–82); 1.29 (Schmid 121f.100–11). See also this translation, note to 115ff.1–39. Boethius, *De institutione musica* (in Friedlein edition just cited), 5.10 (Schmid 33.29–36); 5.9 (Schmid 45.14–47.39); 2.20 (Schmid 116.*descriptio* I [fig. 40]); 3.1 (Schmid 128.222f.); 1.32 (Schmid 132.286–93); 2.18 (Schmid 132f.295–311). Cassiodorus, *Institutiones,* ed. R. A. B. Mynors (Oxford: Clarendon Press, 1937) 2.3.6 and 2.3.21 (Schmid 107.160f); 2.3.5 (Schmid 119.60–5); 2.4.5 (Schmid 121.91–6).

4. These borrowings occur at 33.27, 107f.172–4, 114.264–77, and 125.172f., respectively.

mid–ninth-century date of origin[5]—the first fixed-pitch notation, the earliest (and sometimes only) notated versions of the chants cited, the earliest description of polyphonic singing, and the first technical discussion of modal theory based on final and ambitus.

Dating: Preliminary Observations

The earliest source for one of the *Enchiriadis* treatises, *We,* contains only a small fragment of SE from late ninth-century Werden; the first more or less complete source is the tenth-century manuscript *A,* originally from St.-Amand. Thus, the dates and provenance of the *Enchiriadis* treatises are still a matter of conjecture. A date much before 850 is unlikely for ME, if, as has been argued, the *De institutione musica* of Boethius began to be studied only in the second quarter of the ninth century.[6] Boethius's was the most difficult and technical of all the known Latin treatments of music theory and would have required time to digest, yet ME's author shows great savvy in his use of it. Since SE relies much more on the *De institutione arithmetica,* which in the early ninth century was better known than Boethius's treatise on music, it is not inconceivable that SE could have originated before ME.

However, ME as we know it may not be in its original form. The so-called *Inchiriadon,*[7] a late recension of ME, is likely based on an early version of ME; its use of Boethius is less technical than either ME or SE, and parts of it or its original model could easily have arisen before 850. Thus, using the degree of technical content based on Boethius as a criterion, one could as-

5. Although most scholars have dated the *Enchiriadis* treatises in the tenth or, more recently, in the late ninth century, Nancy Phillips, "*Musica* and *Scolica Enchiriadis:* The Literary, Theoretical, and Musical Sources" (Ph.D. diss., New York University, 1984), p. 511 (henceforth, Phillips *Sources*), notes that "none of the evidence . . . requires a date so late in the [ninth] century." Her analysis of the content of the treatises has led her to postulate that "either or both of the treatises could have been written in the middle of the century, or even slightly earlier" (p. 516).

6. Marie-Elisabeth Duchez, "Jean Scot Eriugène premier lecteur du *De institutione musica* de Boèce?" in *Eriugena: Studien zu seinen Quellen,* ed. Werner Beierwaltes (Heidelberg: Carl Winter Universitätsverlag, 1980), p. 166.

7. Schmid, pp. 187–205. It carries the title *Inchiriadon Uchubaldi Francigenae* and is followed by a tract *De organo,* which describes a style of organum more advanced than that of ME. Much of the *Inchiriadon* has direct parallels with chapters 1–10 of ME, although the ordering and wording of passages common to both works are somewhat different. For more on the *Inchiriadon,* see Heinrich Sowa, "Textvariationen zur Musica Enchiriadis," *Zeitschrift für Musikwissenschaft* 17 (1935):194–207; Phillips *Sources,* pp. 96–106; and Hans Schmid, "Zur sogenannten Pariser Bearbeitung der Musica Enchiriadis," in *Tradition und Wertung: Festschrift für Franz Brunhölzl zum 65. Geburtstag* (Signaringen: Jan Thorbecke, 1989), pp. 211–8.

sign the model for the *Inchiriadon* and also for Aurelian's *Musica disciplina* to a period before the intensive study of *De institutione musica,* whereas ME and Hucbald's *De harmonica institutione* clearly manifest themselves as products of that study. These and other factors will be considered in due course.

Authorship

The question of who wrote the *Enchiriadis* treatises remains unanswered. A number of factors indicate, however, that ME and SE have different authors.[8] It is also possible that one or both may have more than one author. Although it seems certain that the treatises are products of a single intellectual and musical milieu—different in various degrees from, say, that of Aurelian, *Alia Musica,* or Hucbald[9]—many subtle differences in the texts indicate different authorship.

For example, ME (5.52f.) speaks of "the tetrachord of the *graves*" but SE (83.337) of "the *grave* tetrachord," and ME of *neuma* but SE of *neuma regularis* for the same melody.[10] The use of the term *tonus* with respect to "mode" is somewhat different in the two treatises,[11] and the change of locus for the organal voice described in chapter 18 of ME has no parallel in SE. Phrases like *absolute canendo* (33.41) and *mutatio mirabilis* (34.44) are missing in SE (the absence of the latter phrase especially notable since SE uses both words independently). On a larger scale, there is in SE, part 1, an emphasis on pentachords that does not exist in ME, and there are differences in the forms and details of the illustrations. There is also an aura of piety in SE that is not found in ME. SE's author is not content to view the quadrivium primarily as the path to philosophy—as do Boethius explicitly and ME's author implicitly (chapter 18)—but finds its existence a reason for thanking and praising God.[12]

Finally, the term *organum* is not used in exactly the same way in the two treatises. In ME it is equated with both "two-voice song" or *diaphonia* (37.7) and the organal voice (39.5ff.); in SE, *organum* is never actually de-

---

8. For a survey of the views on the question of authorship, see Phillips *Sources,* pp. 396–410. The various attributions in the MS tradition are likely false, so the treatises are considered here to be anonymous. Phillips *Sources,* pp. 397–401, also thinks that the authors of ME and SE are different and gives examples of the differences in style.

9. See below, under "The Enchiriadis Treatises in Relation to Other Pre-Guidonian Sources."

10. See the translation, note to 14.5.

11. See the translation, note to 13.1f.

12. See 107f.169–74 and note to 107f.172–4.

fined, appears only three times, and refers only to the organal voice or its function (for example, 95.46).

The Titles

The commonly used title *Musica enchiriadis* for the first of the two treatises translated here actually has little historical justification. In fact, the evidence suggests that the work bore no title in its earliest stage. The title that Schmid uses at the head of his edition, *Liber enchiriadis de musica,* does occur in several sources,[13] although *enchiriadis* presents other problems, being an apparent corruption of some form of *encheiridion,* the Greek word for manual or handbook, or possibly the medieval form of that word.[14] But regardless of what title, if any, the treatise may have originally had, what we call *Musica enchiriadis* was clearly intended to be a handbook for singers, providing not only practical information but also rationalizations of contemporary performance practices.

The title *Scolica enchiriadis de musica,* on the other hand, appears quite consistently in the MS tradition, although the early manuscripts *A* and *K* (only) have *Scola.*[15] The plural term *scolica,* again of Greek derivation, carries the connotation "excerpts,"[16] and, indeed, it has already been noted

---

13. Schmid 3, critical notes, indicates that this title appears only in two manuscripts (in one instance a later addition) and that fifteen manuscripts, including the early *A,* have no title.

14. Phillips *Sources,* 379f. Phillips infers the latter possibility from Robert Browning, *Medieval and Modern Greek* (London: Hutchinson, 1969), although she wrongly interprets *enchiriadis* as a genitive plural ("of the handbooks"). David Schulenberg (private communication) has suggested that *enchiriadis* might be a latinized feminine genitive singular from *encheirias,* a non-existent word formed by the confusion of *encheiria* and *encheiresis* (both implying "taking in hand"). Schmid, 60, critical note to title of SE, proposes *enchiridiadis,* found in the tenth-century MS H, as probably a transliteration of the Greek adjective ἐφχειριδιώδης. Nonetheless, it seems highly unlikely that the authors of the Enchiriadis treatises knew Greek.

15. Schmid 60, critical notes to title. A large group of manuscripts has *de arte musica* and there are a few other variants, but Schmid indicates that only one source lacks a title altogether.

16. The ninth-century *Scolica graecarum glossarium,* consisting of notes on lectures on the Greek language, defines *scolica* as "proper and briefly excerpted treatments of a subject" (*Scolica dicuntur causae summatim excerptae et propriae*). See M. L. W. Laistner, "Notes on Greek from the Lectures of a Ninth-Century Monastery Teacher," *Bulletin of the John Rylands Library* 7 (1923):433. See also Isidore of Seville on the three types of written works: "The first kind are excerpts, which are called *scholia* in Greek. In them, those things that are perceived to be obscure and difficult are made succinct and brief" (*Primum genus excerpta sunt, quae Graece scholia nuncupantur; in quibus ea quae videntur obscura vel difficilia summatim ac breviter praestringuntur*), Isidore of Seville, *Etymologiarum sive originum libri XX,* ed. W. M. Lindsay (Oxford: Clarendon Press, 1911), 6.8.1. (The other two types of written works defined by Isidore are homilies and "tomes, which we call books or volumes.") The *Scolica graecarum glossarium* has numerous direct quotations from Isidore.

that SE contains many direct quotations and close paraphrases of other sources. However, another explanation for the title is that there was a direct model for it: in one of its MS traditions the *Rhetoric* of Fortunatianus has the title *Scolica enchiriadis*.[17] The possible connection is strengthened in that the *Rhetoric* is also in dialogue form, begins in similar fashion to SE,[18] and includes excerpts from a variety of (unnamed) authors. Moreover, this treatise is also found in an early source (manuscript *H*) containing both ME and SE. Thus, *Scolica enchiriadis* carries the dual implications of "excerpts" and "handbook." Of course, ME, since it also contains quotations and paraphrases, could also qualify for this title, since dialogue format is not implied by either *Scolica* or *enchiriadis*.

ORGANIZATION

Musica enchiriadis

ME is a remarkably cogent, concise, original, and carefully argued document. In terms of content, it is organized in two large parts, with an epilogue. The first nine chapters contain basic definitions and concepts concerning monophonic chant, with particular emphasis on a method of notation, on modality, and on grammatical analogies between language and music. The second large section, chapters 10–18, concerns the perfect consonances or "symphonies" and their application to improvised polyphonic singing, called *diaphonia* or *organum*. Finally, there is a strange concluding nineteenth chapter, related in spirit to the closing passage of chapter 18 and, as we shall see, possibly not the concluding chapter of ME after all, in which the Orpheus myth is reinterpreted and the mysterious power of music celebrated.

The very opening of ME anticipates the structure of the entire treatise: it is stated that the larger constructs of music (like those of language) are the result of successively compounding single elements. What unfolds in the course of the chapters that follow is an explanation of how this successive compounding is done or may be analyzed. In chapters 1–9 the concern is melodic or "horizontal" constructs. First, four discrete pitches (the four finals) are combined to form a tetrachord that both governs all the modes

---

17. The first to note this connection was Phillip Spitta, "Die *Musica enchiriadis* und ihr Zeitalter," *Vierteljahrsschrift für Musikwissenschaft* 5 (1889):467. For a more up-to-date discussion see Phillips *Sources*, pp. 381–4.

18. "Quid est rhetorica? Bene dicendi scientia. Quid est orator? Vir bonus dicendi peritus." (What is rhetoric? The science of speaking properly. What is an orator? A good man skilled in speaking.) Karl Halm, ed., *Rhetores latini minores* (Leipzig: Teubner, 1863), p. 81. For more on rhetoric, see "Grammar and Rhetoric" below.

and can be replicated, yielding in the process the pitch-set of the *Enchiriadis* scale. Then is shown how modal melodies are compounded of musico-grammatical phrases (*comma, colon, particula*). Chapters 10–18, in turn, treat the harmonic or "vertical" compounds of tones—from the symphonies of individual pitches to the simultaneously sounding melodies of organum, which represents the highest degree of complexity.

An important feature of the treatise is its balance between theoretical and practical. Once the *Enchiriadis* scale and notation are explained (chaps. 1–3) and the modes are defined in terms of final and ambitus (chaps. 4–5), the focus shifts in characteristically Carolingian fashion to the practical: how to recognize by ear the identity of any tetrachordal step by its intervallic context (chaps. 6–7). Practical exercises are provided. It is stressed that the key to identifying any individual step is knowing its relation to proximate semitones.

In chapter 8, this is given visual expression by a series of diagrams designed as a set of parallel lines ("as it were, strings"), each line preceded by the appropriate daseian sign.[19] A melody is then given in successively higher transpositions, resulting in a different final (and a different interval series) for each transposition. Then four pairs of antiphons, one pair for each final, are used to illustrate and contrast authentic and plagal melodies. In all this, modal differences can be perceived by singing, hearing and seeing.

The "preliminary exercises, as it were, and basic beginnings" having been covered, some essential technical terminology is now introduced (chap. 9): defined are the technical musical terms *harmonia, sonus, phthongus, tonus, epogdous; semitonium, limma* or *diesis;* the mathematical proportions *sescupla,*[20] *sesquialter, hemiola, sesquitertia; modi* or *tropi;* the grammatical/rhetorical terms *particula, comma* and *colon;* and two more musical terms, *diastema* and *systema.* With the return at the end of chapter 9 to certain terms and concepts not encountered since the opening of chapter 1, the overall shape of this first part of ME, which concerns plainchant, is nicely rounded off. On the other hand, an adumbration of the discussion of organum to follow may be seen in the definitions of mathematical proportions that are mentioned for the first time in the treatise.

The second large section of ME comprises chapters 10–12, which define the perfect consonances or symphonies (*symphoniae*), and chapters 13–18, covering the theory and practice of organum. The symphonies are divided

---

19. The text implies that originally the lines were drawn in four different colors, one for each tetrachordal step.

20. The term *sescuplus* has two meanings in the *Enchiriadis* treatises. See the end of "The Harmonics Tradition" below.

into simple (diatessaron, diapente, and diapason) and composite (the simple symphonies expanded by an octave). Simultaneous (*in unum*) sounding is not a necessary condition here, although it is not precluded; at issue are harmonic distances, not performance practices.

The discussion of organum itself proceeds with the expected logic and rigor we now expect of ME. First, simple organum at the fourth is introduced (with an example, however, that avoids problematic intervals dealt with later), then organum at the fourth with octave doublings. Chapter 15 takes up doubled organum at the fifth (simple organum at the fifth presents no problems, as was already implied in chap. 12). At chapter 17, ME takes up the problem cleverly circumvented in the example in chapter 13: that the fourth below a deuterus tone (the second lowest tone of a tetrachord) is a tritone, not a diatessaron. For this reason the organal voice follows "a certain law of its own" to preclude circumstances that would cause a tritone to sound. Thus the range of the added voice in organum at the fourth may be compressed to the interval of a third or fourth; however, when the principal melody has a sufficiently wide range, this situation can be mitigated by shifting the locus of the organal voice as the principal voice moves into higher and lower regions of the pitch spectrum (chap. 18).

This second main part of ME also contains two quotations from the *De institutione musica* of Boethius, tellingly adduced in chapters 11 and 16 to anticipate possible objections against the practice of doubling tones at the eleventh as can happen in doubled organum. The author carefully extracts passages from Boethius (both based on Ptolemy) that serve his purpose, not bothering to mention that elsewhere in *De institutione musica* are statements contradictory to Ptolemy's position.[21]

Chapter 19 has been the subject of much speculation. In its philosophical tone and avoidance of technical material and jargon it continues the spirit of the conclusion to chapter 18, but for that reason seems redundant. Indeed, Jacques Handschin suggested that it was a later addition to ME.[22] The opening of the chapter, referring to the ancient musical myth of Orpheus, is not atypical for an introductory chapter in a medieval music treatise, although the allegorical interpretation offered is. Furthermore, the chapter's conclusion, indicating that a Boethian exposition of the mathematical foundations of music follows, could reasonably refer to the main body of a work to which chapter 19 is the prologue. In fact, the more mathematically oriented SE nor-

21. Boethius, *De inst. mus.* 2.27 and 1.5 (Friedlein 259.15–9 and 192.26–193.1), represents the opinion of the Pythagoreans that the eleventh is not a consonance because its ratio 8:3 is not a multiple or superparticular.

22. Jacques Handschin, "Die Musikanschauung des Johannes Scotus," *Vierteljahrsschrift für Literaturwissenschaft und Geisteswissenschaft* 5 (1927):321 n. 1.

mally follows ME in the MS sources. It would be unusual for a treatise the size of SE not to have some sort of preamble.

The manuscript tradition does not support this hypothesis, for in only one source does this chapter not close ME. However, since the oldest manuscripts are at the very least one generation removed from the original state of the text, there is no certainty that chapter 19 or even the closing passage of chapter 18—both so different in style from the rest of ME—was originally part of the treatise; moreover, chapter 19 is also not part of the *Inchiriadon*.

I tend to the interpretation[23] that the closing passage of chapter 18 (56.49–61) makes a fitting conclusion to ME, that chapter 19 really belongs to SE, and that at some early stage of the MS tradition the misalignment was introduced. However, the possibility can also be raised of a hypothetical SE that had chapter 19 as a prologue; we will return to this briefly after considering the organization of that treatise.

Scolica enchiriadis

The most striking feature of the *Scolica* is its dialogue form. This style is not necessarily associated with a medieval *scolica*, although the Fortunatianus *De rhetorica* from which SE's name may be derived, is, in fact, a dialogue. The literary dialogue format was, of course, established by Plato, who modeled it on the teaching method of his teacher Socrates. Since then, dialogue has frequently been employed in didactic works, including Augustine's *De musica*. In fact, it was *De musica* that probably inspired the form of SE, for both the opening definition of music and the materials for the discussion of rhythm at the end of Part 1 are drawn from it.[24]

SE is divided into three numbered parts of unequal length. Part 1 (429 lines in Schmid's edition) opens with a traditional definition of music; it then discourses extensively, aided by examples in daseian notation, on correct and incorrect singing (focusing particularly on how errors come about by misplacing the semitone) and on various aspects of modality; finally, it closes with a passage on rhythmic performance as an embellishment of the chant. In part 2 (284 lines), the first half is devoted to the symphonies and organum, the second half to an introduction to quadrivial studies (based largely on Cassiodorus and Boethius), with an assertion of the fundamental importance of number for music (supported by a citation from Augustine's *De ordine*). This division in the middle of part 2 amounts to a logical (but not formal) partition of the materials of SE, between the "how" and the "why."[25]

Part 3 (655 lines) is devoted mainly to a discussion of number theory based principally on Boethius and Cassiodorus. The various classes of inequality, their correspondences in musical intervals, why only six ratios produce musical consonances, and definitions of the arithmetic, harmonic, and geometric means are taken up, supported by instructions on how to demonstrate the principles involved with pipes and strings. At the end, attention is refocused on practical music in relation to the *Enchiriadis* scale and notation; taken up are modal differences of tetrachords, likeness at the fifth degree, and the need to preserve consonance when singing in octaves (which requires the added voice to employ pitches outside the *Enchiriadis* scale). The treatise then ends abruptly.

Partly because of sheer size, SE is the more difficult treatise to read and digest. However, it has been claimed that SE has a pedagogical logic no less convincing than that of ME.[26] In view of the overall structure of the treatise and various "road signs" along one's traversal of it (giving present position and announcing what lies ahead), this view is certainly defensible.

Nevertheless, there are many frustrating organizational aspects of the treatise as well. Near the beginning of part 1 the master tells the disciple that a skilled and learned singer (*peritus cantor*) must understand the properties of individual pitches, the rhythmical aspects of chant performance, and other unspecified things external to the science of music (*extrinsecus occurrentes,* 61.14 and 89.424f.) that nonetheless bear on musical performance.[27] One might expect that the three-part division of the treatise would correspond to this threefold division of what it is necessary to know. Yet this is not the case.[28] To be sure, the pitch set (with corresponding notation) and rhythmic performance are taken up in that order, but both within part 1. However, just what constitutes the *extrinsecus occurrentes,* or matters external—accidental, one could say—to the science of singing, remains problematic. It has been proposed, for example, that the phrase *extrinsecus occurrentes* refers to the practice of organum,[29] an optional and improvisatory manner of performance, although some medieval readers thought that this phrase referred to such matters as the quality of a singer's voice. But there still remains better than half of the treatise to be accounted for, and the materials in this latter half deal with the most fundamental issues, such as the numerical basis of music—hardly something that qualifies as *extrinsecus.*

26. Phillips *Sources*, pp. 152, 159.

27. See the translation, note to 61.14.

28. Moreover, that SE is, practically speaking, divided into "how" and "why" halves is not indicated in the treatise itself. See note to 106.141ff.

29. Phillips *Sources*, p. 146; but see the translation, note to Schmid 61.14.

The reader's problems with SE are not limited to large-scale organization. There are a wordiness and even an inaccuracy not present in ME, and many awkward moments. At 128.216, SE implies that the 8:3 ratio (the eleventh) is a dissonance, although this undermines the argument elsewhere for the legitimacy of organum at the fourth and contradicts the opening of part 2, where the diapason-plus-diatessaron is classed as a symphony. When the Disciple asks (102.75ff.) what is different about the first composite form of the diapente (fig. 29) and the second form of the diatessaron (fig. 35), he receives the seemingly irrelevant answer that the organal voice at the fourth follows its own laws and stands still; the confusion is resolved only when the reader realizes that the ill-formulated question has less to do with composite forms of fourth and fifth than with the behavior of the organal voice. In part 2 (103.93) the Master flatly states that tropes or modes "always recur" at the fifth step (correct) and the eighth step (wrong, since the *Enchiriadis* scale is not periodic at the octave), without saying that replication at the octave necessitates at times going outside the scale.[30] There are still other examples.

That the largest section of the treatise, part 3, is not anticipated by anything in part 1 (which clearly spells out the categories of practical knowledge in which the *peritus cantor* must be expert) raises the question of whether parts 1 and 3 originated independently of each other. Part 3, in fact, seems to come much closer to satisfying the expectations raised by chapter 19 of ME, where it is stated that "that most eminent author Boethius relates many marvelous things about the principles of music, proving all of them simply by the authority of numbers. Of this, if God grant it, the little work following will contain some portion." This description applies only to the bulk of part 3 of SE and to some of the second half of part 2, which ends very similarly to chapter 19: "But I pray you to undertake to treat more fully the nature of numbers and to repeat certain things that have been said before, so that by reflecting on them I may somehow arrive at the inner secret of the basis of music by means of the authority of numbers."

Although there is no evidence in the extant MSS to support it, one could hypothesize that the first half of SE (to 105.140) was written independently,

---

30. To put it another way, SE's author describes what happens in practice rather than what the *Enchiriadis* scale and notation allow. It is only at the end of part 3 that it is made clear that, in doubling a melody at the octave, maintaining the distance of a duple proportion (that is, a perfect octave) is more important than adhering to the pitch set of the daseian scale. ME is much more forthright on this problem: it bluntly states that tones eight steps apart can be made consistently perfect only by means of a "wondrous change" (*mutatione mirabili*, 34.44), that is, by going outside the daseian framework.

perhaps in two parts, the second being the teaching on organum. Thereby would have been treated the three areas of expertise required of the *peritus cantor* (if one interprets *extrinsecus occurrentes* as organum). Either before this or afterward, chapter 19 of ME and part 3 of SE (up to 147.549) were written, the former serving as prologue to the latter, both together perhaps serving as a companion piece to ME, providing the mathematical foundations missing in it. At some point the standard arrangement of the treatises came into being, with the second half of SE's part 2—its ending modeled on the conclusion of ME's chapter 19, which it now replaced—written to create a smooth transition to what now was part 3 of SE, which was extended by the material after 147.549 to make a connection with the content of part 1. (This material does not require all the preceding harmonics information as theoretical underpinning.)

On the other hand, the phrase *vir bonus,* which appears in chapter 19 of ME (57.5), may have been inspired by the Fortunatianus *De rhetorica,*[31] the title and opening of which have correspondences with SE, part 1. Furthermore, the phrase *magisterio numerorum* appears in chapter 19 as well as at the end of part 2 (59.38 and 115.281f.). This may point to a common origin for chapter 19 of ME and parts 1 and 2 of SE.

THE TEACHINGS OF THE *ENCHIRIADIS* TREATISES

The *Enchiriadis* Scale and Notation

The first order of business in ME is the description of a scale and notation that are found only in a small number of treatises of the ninth and tenth centuries. The steps of the scale,[32] selected from a theoretically infinite series by the criterion of the adult male vocal range, are grouped into four disjunct tone–semitone–tone tetrachords, with two further steps, *residui,* added at the top.[33] The number of these steps is eighteen, the same as in the combined Greater and Lesser Perfect Systems of ancient Greek theory, but their names and disposition differ from the Greek tradition. The groups of four steps are called, respectively, *graves, finales, superiores* and *excellentes,* of which the *finales* are the starting point; the individual steps of each tetrachord are

31. Phillips *Sources,* p. 391. See also note 18 above.

32. Because of the ambiguity of the word "tone," which can refer to a discrete pitch, the interval of a whole tone, or a mode, the term "step" will be used here for the first of these meanings. "Step" also conveys better the abstract sense of relative position than "pitch," which might suggest a specific (absolute) pitch level to some readers.

33. See ME, chapters 1 and 2 (4.15–7.17) and SE, part 1 (62.35–63.42 and 83.336–84.347).

named, in ascending order, *protus* (first), *deuterus* (second), *tritus* (third), and *tetrardus* (fourth).

The tetrachordal steps are represented by signs that incorporate a symbol in the shape of a *daseia* or ⅂, a grammatical accent mark. By modifying the daseia by the addition of other shapes like a *C* and an *S*, or by simplifying the daseia into an *iota*-like slanted line, a set of four basic signs is created for the finales steps: ⌐ ⌐ ⌡ ⌐. The individual symbols are rotated to generate the signs for the corresponding steps of the other tetrachords. Significantly, the signs for tritus, the step that in ascending is always a semitone above the step below,[34] do not adhere consistently to this principle.

The *Enchiriadis* pitch set is not octave-based, for perfect octaves do not occur throughout its extent. For example, B♭ to b♮ and F♯ to f♮ occur eight steps apart. The system is thus imperfectly capable of representing either organum at the fourth or the octave doublings that are clearly a part of organal singing. Since the value of the *Enchiriadis* treatises is often judged to reside in the first descriptions of polyphony they contain, the incongruity between the *Enchiriadis* scale and organum has seemed inexplicable until recently. It is only with the hypothesis of Nancy Phillips that a reasonable explanation has been offered: that the *Enchiriadis* scale likely corresponds to the pitches actually used in ninth-century chant. When this pitch set gave way, beginning in the eleventh century, to that of the emerging octave-based modal theory, older melodies were made to conform to the new pitch arrangement.[35]

The limitations of the *Enchiriadis* scale for organum and octave singing are reflected especially in the illustrations that accompany the discussion of these subjects. The authors of the treatises resort to a variety of means to make their points when the daseian notation proves inadequate to the task; this results in various alternative or supplementary ways of indicating harmonic relationships—for example, through Roman letters (as in figs. 10.4 and 11.2 of ME and fig. 27 of ME), Roman numerals (figs. 29ff. of SE), and even geometrical diagrams (for example, fig. 11.1 of ME) from which harmonic spacing can be inferred. The exposition of the *Enchiriadis* scale and notation is quite succinct and straightforward in ME, but is accomplished in several stages in SE, with the pupil shown the full set of tones, tetrachords,

---

34. The position of tritus is so formulated here because of the way it is treated in SE, part 1, when various errors resulting from singing tones not in the *Enchiriadis* scale are illustrated. There the tritus symbol represents an ascending semitone. See, for example, figs. 7b, 10b, 11b, and 13b.

35. See Nancy Phillips, "The Dasia Notation and Its Manuscript Tradition," in *Musicologie médiévale: notations et séquences* (Paris: Librairie Honoré Champion, 1987), pp. 157–73; and Phillips *Sources*, chap. 11.

and notational signs only after considerable practice with a small subset of the note forms (and not even all of that is explained to him at first).

THE THEORY OF THE MODES

The *Enchiriadis* treatises are notable for transmitting one of the earliest states of the theory of the ecclesiastical modes. Early evidence for the modes exists in eighth-century tonaries and in Aurelian's *Musica disciplina*. What ME and SE offer, however, is a more technical description of the modes and hence more specific information about the musical criteria of modal classification than in earlier sources.

The modal teachings of the *Enchiriadis* treatises are centered around two theoretical concepts: the notions of final and of ambitus or melodic range. There is no discussion of octave species, or indeed of a theoretical octave ambitus, so basic to later definitions of mode. Similarly, there is no discussion of psalm-tone formulas, although SE (73.166–75.193) is particularly concerned with the proper joining of melodic segments. There is no mention of modes other than the standard eight, such as the *parapteres* or additional modes attributed by Aurelian to Charlemagne.[36] Both ME and SE, however, cite names of the Byzantine modal formulas and make use of similar formulas (*neuma, neuma regularis*) for the purpose of demonstration (14.5, 8, 11 and 77.215f.).

The following summarizes the modal theory of the *Enchiriadis* treatises:

1. There are four finals (protus, deuterus, tritus and tetrardus), each of which gives its name to and presides over an authentic and a plagal mode. The finals correspond to the modern scale steps D, E, F, and G.

2. The final is the primary determinant of mode and is so called because every proper melody ends on one of these four steps.

3. The authentic modes are referred to as *autentus* and *maior* in both treatises and in SE also as *auctoralis* (82.310); the plagals are referred to as *plagis, minor,* and *subiugalis* and in SE also as *lateralis* (82.311).

4. A mode is referred to variously as *tropus, tonus,* and *modus.* Only the first of these terms is used exclusively with that meaning. Moreover, both treatises indicate that *tonus* is not a proper term for mode, despite long-standing usage.[37]

5. Because of the structure of the *Enchiriadis* scale, steps separated by a fifth (SE: *sociales,* 82.318f., and *compares,* 73.159f.) have the same name and character; hence, (only) melodies transposed by a fifth maintain the same mode. SE also speaks of a special relationship between steps a fourth apart (*compares,* 82.320f.).

---

36. See the article "Parapter" by Charles Atkinson in *HdMT* (1978). Aurelian's account appears in chapter 8 of his *Musica disciplina.* Cf. also "The *Enchiriadis* Treatises in Relation to Other Pre-Guidonian Sources" below.

37. See the translation, notes to 13.1f. and 105.132.

6. Authentic and plagal modes with the same final are differentiated by their ranges: the accepted lower boundary for both is a fifth below the final, whereas the upper boundary is a ninth above the final for the authentic and a fifth above the final for the plagal (9.9f., 9.1–5, 85.365–71).

7. In chapter 19 of ME, it is stated that some subjects may be expressible in any mode but that others require specific modes for their proper expression.

8. In ME (only), passing reference is made (22.20) to the Dorian, Phrygian, and Lydian modes, but these are not further identified.[38]

THE THEORY OF ORGANUM

The *Enchiriadis* treatises are the oldest sources of information regarding polyphonic performance. However, polyphony is not treated as an innovation but as something already established: ME says it is properly called *diaphony* but "customarily" referred to as *organum* (37.6–8); SE does not see the need even to define the term. Treated as a middle ground between monophony and organum is singing in octaves, something that occurs naturally and does not require training (47.1–3), as when men and boys sing together (28.3–5 and 102.75–7). However, since octave doubling is apparently a regular part of organal performance, such doublings are also considered in the discussion of organum (41f.19ff.).

In the *Enchiriadis* treatises, *organum* refers to improvised singing at a fourth or fifth below the given melody; the principal and organal voices are respectively designated *vox principalis* and *vox organalis* (for example, 49.18f. and 92.30f.), although the term *organum* is also used to mean "organal voice" (38.2, 39.5, etc.). The texts and illustrations concerning organum indicate that it is possible to double or even triple (91f.20f.) either or both voices.

Because the *Enchiriadis* scale has periodicity at the fifth, organum at the fifth can be perfectly performed and represented within the daseian framework. However, the same is true neither for octave doubling nor for organum at the fourth. Thus, parallel perfect octaves are consistently obtainable only by a "wondrous change" (*mutatio mirabilis*, 34.44), and organum at the fourth must proceed by "a law of its own" (48.13) or by "natural law" (97.54f.). This law, treated in chapter 18 of ME and at 102.89ff., puts a limit on how low the organal voice may begin or end. That limit is the tetrardus of the tetrachord below that of the principal voice. The *necessary* result is

---

38. However, in the *Inchiriadon* (204.*descriptio* 14) these names, plus Mixolydian, are associated with the modal scales built on protus, deuterus, tritus, and tetrardus, respectively. But this clearly represents a later reworking of the modal theory of ME, for it also involves association with octave species.

oblique motion, which undermines the validity of the modern term "parallel organum" for the practice of the *Enchiriadis* tradition. In chapter 18 ME also shows how the lower limit is simultaneously moved to the next tetrardus when the melody shifts into another register. SE, however, does not describe this practice.

PEDAGOGICAL METHODS, INSTRUMENTS,
AND PERFORMANCE PRACTICES

The *Enchiriadis* treatises not only offer a theoretical framework for ninth-century musical practice; they also provide practical learning exercises, demonstrations with pipes and strings (in SE[39]), and information concerning rhythm, tempo, and performing forces. Furthermore, the chants chosen to illustrate organum tell us something about the liturgical context for early polyphony.

Exercises

Both treatises give the singer an opportunity to practice what is taught, and both have a concern for correctness of modality in singing, which means recognizing the quality of each of the four basic steps of the *Enchiriadis* tetrachords. This is a matter of knowing where each step (in whatever tetrachord) is located relative to the nearest semitones. SE goes into this matter more deeply than ME, providing in part 1 not only exercises for practicing the correct placement of the various scale degrees but also several demonstrations, using "ladder" diagrams, that illustrate how the semitone intervals can be misplaced.[40] In similar fashion, when the symphony of the diatessaron is taught before organum is described, the student has the opportunity to sing the diatessaron both by skip and as a series of four consecutive pitches (24.*descriptio* 1 [fig. 10.1]). Again, the organum diagrams are there not only for study, but for singing during the learning process, even though organum was an improvisational art and was not performed from score (as was, for example, the later organum of the Notre Dame School).

Demonstrations

The demonstration of theoretical principles through sounding media was not new in the ninth century; it is implicit in the famous but apocryphal

39. Phillips *Sources*, p. 155 n. 47, isolates six "tracts" within SE that use instruments to illustrate harmonic principles discussed. They are at 112f.237–58, 133.314–20, 136.364–73, 137.374–81, 145f.512–24, and 146f.530–49.

40. However, it is also stated (70.132–5) that, like a sometimes permissible barbarism or solecism in poetry, normally illegal pitches, that is, those outside the defined scale, may occur in the transposed melodies. For "ladder" diagrams see the note to 67.*descriptio* 7a/b.

story of Pythagoras and the hammers, and explicit in the treatises of Ptolemy and Boethius. But the specific mention of pipes (in addition to the traditional strings) is a reminder that the organ came to the West from Byzantium and was to play an important role in musical pedagogy and practice.[41] According to SE, fixed-pitch instruments are especially useful for demonstration because, once tuned, they do not sound out of tune as voices often do (61.23–5). The use of instruments in teaching is especially evident in the second half of SE, where specific points of theory are supported by pipe and string measurements; the fact that some of the harmonic divisions result in what we call today a C-major scale may be directly tied to the organ, for Hucbald too has such a scale, which he says reflects the tuning of the organ.[42]

Performance Media

Organum is primarily but not exclusively a type of vocal improvisation. Although the basic texture is that of two adult male soloists, boys' voices are explicitly mentioned in connection with singing in double octaves (28.4) and in organum with upper-octave doublings (40f.19f., 102.75f.). Moreover, a wide variety of combinations of principal and organal voices, which may be doubled or replaced by instruments, is indicated (39.5–40.14 and in many examples in ME and in part 2 of SE).

Rhythm and Tempo

The temporal aspects of music are also considered by the *Enchiriadis* treatises. Thereby is provided important, if not very complete, information concerning certain aspects of ninth-century performance practice. Both treatises use the terms *modesta morositas* to describe the slow tempo appropriate to organum performance (38.14f. and 97.56), implying perhaps that monophonic performance of chant was faster than organum. There are also statements, however, that the tempo of the chant may be fast or slow (88.406) and that this is a function of "time, place, and outside conditions" (89.424f.). SE gives a long, if frustratingly imprecise, description of measured rhythm as a normal, temporal embellishment of the chant (86.383–89.427), obviously drawing on the early books of St. Augustine's *De musica*. From SE's teachings all that can really be learned is that rhythmic values can be double or half the basic unit, and that this is most likely to occur at the ends (and be-

41. The gift of an organ to Pepin in 757 was a widely chronicled event; in the second quarter of the ninth century a great organ was constructed in Aachen for Louis the Pious. Peter Williams, "Organ," *The New Grove Dictionary of Music and Musicians* (London: Macmillan, 1980), 13:727.

42. For the "C-major" divisions, see 145.*descriptio* 4 (fig. 43) and 147.*descriptio* 5 (fig. 44) in SE, part 3. For Hucbald, see GS 1:110b, trans. Warren Babb, in *Hucbald, Guido, and John on Music* (New Haven and London: Yale University Press, 1978), pp. 25 and 24, fig. 6.

ginnings) of phrases. The treatment of rhythm comes before the exposition of organum in SE, and there is no hint to whether it also applies to organal performance; the statement that measured rhythm is used whether one or more voices is involved (88.406f.) could, of course, apply to solo or choral monophony.

Liturgical Context

Finally, there is the matter of performance context. Here the choice of chants to exemplify the modes and organal performance is striking: there are no Mass chants whatsoever, and the vast majority of examples are drawn from the canonical repertory of the Office.[43] The examples chosen to illustrate organum include two psalm tones, the *Te Deum,* and the versus *Rex caeli.*[44] From this it would appear that polyphony was far more likely to embellish Matins than Mass.

INTELLECTUAL AND CULTURAL INFLUENCES ON THE *ENCHIRIADIS* TREATISES

Grammar and Rhetoric

It would be difficult to overestimate the importance of grammar in the Carolingian era.[45] As the West emerged from the Dark Ages around the beginning of the ninth century, there began a revival of learning and education—the "Carolingian Renaissance" it is often called—that was launched by an ambitious and aspiring Charlemagne under the supervision of Alcuin of York. Charlemagne, for whom the Christian religion was as much a political tool to unify his empire as it was the basis of his genuine piety, saw his most urgent tasks to be the producing of well-educated clergy able to spread the Gospel with uniformity and the training of civil servants qualified to administer his empire. This resulted in tremendous emphasis being placed, at first, on the basics—reading, writing and arithmetic[46]—which could be followed by study of more theoretical, systematic works such as the grammatical trea-

43. "The musical examples of the *Enchiriadis* treatises comprise nine antiphons, two psalm tones, a portion of the *Te Deum,* the noannoeane melody of the first tone, and the first four lines of the versus *Rex caeli*. All but the last two—for which no specific liturgical use was ever designated—are office chants, and except for the antiphon *Ego sum via* these office chants are drawn from the weekly cursus." (Phillips *Sources,* p. 420).

44. See the translation, note to 12.*descriptio* (fig. 7.1).

45. For a detailed consideration of the function of grammatical concepts and terminology in music-theoretic writings of the Middle Ages, see Mathias Bielitz, *Musik und Grammatik* (Munich and Salzburg: Emil Katzbichler, 1977).

46. Arithmetic in elementary education was simple digital calculation, necessary for record keeping and for computing the date of Easter and other feast days.

tises by Priscian, Donatus, and Marius Victorinus and the *Arithmetic* of Boethius. Communicated with the aid of a clear style of script (the Carolingian minuscule) that was a product of the same policy, the Latin language—the language not only of the Bible and scholarship, but also of law, diplomacy, and court records—reacquired in the Carolingian world a general level of correctness and uniformity that had long been lacking.[47]

This renewed importance of grammar is obvious from the very opening of ME. Here the subject of music is introduced by means of a traditional analogy between grammar and music, discrete pitches being likened to the letters of language; from these elemental units the larger constructs of speech and song arise. Then, following the tradition of the grammatical tracts, ME establishes, as it were, the "alphabet" for representing musical sounds; these "letters" (the daseian symbols) are called *notae, figurae, karacteres, signa*—terms also found in grammatical treatises, as is also the *daseia* sign or ⌐, the mark for the aspirated *h*.[48] Although this shape is the same as one of the signs of the Greek notation transmitted by Boethius,[49] it was probably used by the authors of the *Enchiriadis* treatises precisely because it had the shape of the daseia. Hence it would be recognizable to those without familiarity with ancient Greek notation, since all readers would have studied grammar. And indeed it is as the daseia sign that the symbol is described.

The impetus to develop a precise pitch notation for plainchant—first of its kind in the West—may well have grown out of the great concern with uniformity that was part of the Carolingian educational, administrative, and liturgical reforms, which sought to achieve uniformity in many areas of life. In this light, the daseian notation may be regarded as an administrative or legislative tool used for defining the norms and laws of ecclesiastical song, especially with regard to the modal system. Furthermore, it made possible the analysis of chants (and, less successfully, their polyphonic elaborations). However, the notation was too cumbersome to enable the large body of existing chant to be encoded. Thus the plainsong repertory continued to be transmitted orally or in imprecise neumatic notation until at least the mid-

---

47. The teachings of the grammarians were not welcomed enthusiastically by church authorities of earlier times (such as Gregory the Great), who feared the influence of the pagan poetry contained in these treatises. See Detlef Illmer, *Formen der Erziehung und Wissensvermittlung im frühen Mittelalter* (München: Arbeo-Gesellschaft, 1971), pp. 57–73.

48. For example, the fifth-century grammarian Priscian, in his *De accentibus* (GL 3:520.14f.), defines the daseia as the eighth in a series of ten accent marks that also include the acute, grave, circumflex, long, short, hyphen, diastole, apostrophe, and psile. The last named is the daseia reversed, i.e., rotated 180 degrees. Moreover, Priscian, like the later author of ME (3.1–3), notes that, starting from letters, there are successively formed syllables, "parts," and then an oration (GL 3:519.21f.)

49. *De inst. mus.* 4.3–4 (Friedlein, pp. 308–14).

eleventh century, when Guido d'Arezzo's notion of a staff with clef began to take hold.[50]

The reader of ME is told that, although the number of human sounds and pitches is theoretically infinite, the number of letters in the alphabet and of usable pitches is fixed by convention. When the talk turns to the symphonies, in preparation for the explanation of organum, another analogy with grammar is made: just as every combination of letters does not produce a meaningful word, so every combination of pitches does not produce a symphony or perfect consonance. Furthermore, some Latin words that might be thought to have originated in musical discourse are first documented in grammatical treatises; an example is *inconsonus*, initially used for an improper combination of letters, words, and spoken sounds.[51]

If grammar is concerned with the elements that are the foundation of language, rhetoric, another of the verbal arts, deals with larger constructs of language and with matters of style and affect. Thus the authors of the *Enchiriadis* treatises describe the phrase structure of melodies using the same terms employed by grammarians and rhetoricians for the structure of sentences: *comma, colon, particula, membrum, distinctio,* and *periodus* (22.21–4, 50.25, 51.12, and 82.321–33). Even the interchangeability of the terms *colon* and *comma* (22.23f. and 83.332f.) has a precedent in grammatical and rhetorical theory (the terms are proper to both disciplines).[52]

Moreover, in two highly original passages (22f.26–32 and 85.371–3), *diastema* and *systema,* terms of Greek harmonic theory, are defined in an unprecedented way: in connection with both rhetorical theory and musical practice. Diastema is now said to correspond to the musical space occupied by a comma (in the new sense of a short musical phrase) and a systema to that encompassed by an entire melody. Thus there is a bold synthesis of concepts from three separate realms—grammar and rhetoric, harmonics, and plainchant—that clearly distinguishes the pragmatic Carolingian spirit from the more speculative approach of earlier writings from which ME and SE draw so much.

The principal purpose of rhetoric, of course, is oratorical persuasiveness, and that too is mirrored in the *Enchiriadis* treatises. In the middle of chap-

---

50. Reflections on the development of musical notation as a natural expression of the age are found in, among other places, Leo Treitler, "Reading and Singing: On the Genesis of Occidental Music-Writing," *Early Music History* 4 (1984):135–208.

51. The opposite also occurs. Terms like *consonantia* and *dissonantia* are borrowed from music by the grammarians.

52. For example, the African rhetorician Maris Victorinus (mid–fourth century) indicates that *colon* is often used (wrongly) for *comma: abusive autem etiam comma dicitur colon* (GL 6:54.5f.)

ter 19 of SE, attention is focused briefly, but movingly, on the rhetorical aspects of song; the need to match the musical idiom with the subject and affections of the text is stressed, "so that melodies are peaceful in tranquil subjects, joyful in happy matters, somber in sad." Moreover, "there are subjects that simply do not express their content through just any mode," nor do they tolerate transposition from one mode to another. What is somewhat surprising about this passage, however, is that music is described as passive rather than active, merely reflecting rather than also instilling in the listener the emotion embodied in the text. Nonetheless, in the closing paragraph to chapter 18 it had been stated that "the same guiding principle that controls the concord of pitches regulates the natures of mortals"; this clearly implies that music has rhetorical and affective power.

That the Fortunatianus *Rhetoric* may have served as a model for SE has been mentioned above. Not only are its dialogue form and opening lines similar to SE, but the phrase *vir bonus*—which, as the commonly used designation for the ideal orator in rhetorical treatises, means more than simply "a good man"[53]—also occurs in chapter 19 of ME as the translation of the name of Aristeus, who is characterized there as a pursuer of knowledge and understanding represented allegorically by Euridice.[54]

The Influence of Byzantium

During the eighth and ninth centuries there were periods of fairly intense contact between Byzantium and the Franks. There were exchanges of ambassadors and of gifts, and even discussions of intermarriage between the two imperial families. Given the Carolingian interest in the more highly developed culture of the Christian East, it is natural that there was some commerce in information about liturgical and musical practices.

Knowledge of Byzantine-Frankish musical relations is still at a relatively undeveloped state, largely owing to an absence of source material, but it is clear that Carolingian chant theory was not unaffected by the Byzantine tradition with its eight melodic modes (*oktoechoi*). Thus the modal system outlined in the *Enchiriadis* treatises shares with the Eastern system the diatonic genus, four authentic modes (called *kyrioi*, "lords," in the East), and four other modes (called "plagal" in both East and West). The Byzantine system also shares with the *Enchiriadis* teachings a central octave D–d formed

53. See note 18 above.

54. Although Fulgentius is apparently the primary source of both the Orpheus myth and its allegorical interpretation in ME, chapter 19, it should be noted that Aristeus does not figure in Fulgentius's version of the myth. Aristeus is found, however, in Vergil's account (*Georgics* 4.453–527), but is hardly idealized there: according to the poet, Euridice was bitten by the snake while fleeing the lustful Aristeus.

by two disjunct tetrachords of the form TST. The terminological similarities between the two systems extend further to the designations *protos, deuteros, tritos,* and *tetrardos,* each for an authentic/plagal modal pair.[55]

The *Enchiriadis* treatises bear witness to yet another aspect of the Byzantine tradition. The use of a short melodic formula (with the text *Alleluia*) preceding the antiphons in ME, chapter 8, and especially the use of this same formula in SE with the text *Noannoeane* (77f.*descriptiones* 16f. [figs. 16f.]) recall immediately the function of the *echemata* of the Byzantine system, used to introduce the singing of the office hymns known as *troparia.* That these formulas as indicators of mode are modeled on Byzantine practice is also inferrable from Aurelian's oft-cited account of how, when he asked a Greek how to translate these syllables, the Greek responded that they were simply joyful exclamations and could not be translated. In similar fashion ME views these modal "names" "less as meaningful words than as syllables associated with well-formed melody."[56]

There are, of course, differences between the two systems. The central D–d octave of the Byzantine system is extended on either end to encompass the double octave A–a′ by *conjunct* tetrachords and an added step a′ at the top (comparable, but probably not causally related to, the two *residui* in the daseian scale).[57] Melodic formulas are more central to modal classification in the East than in the West, whereas ambitus and final play a greater role in Western than in Eastern modal theory. The numbering of the modes is different: in the Eastern practice, modes 1–4 are the principal modes, modes 5–8 the plagals. The Byzantine modal syllables and formulas are somewhat dif-

---

55. A brief but classic introduction to Byzantine chant theory is Oliver Strunk, "The Tonal System of Byzantine Music," *Musical Quarterly* 28 (1942): 190–204, reprinted in Oliver Strunk, *Essays on Music in the Byzantine World* (New York: Norton, 1977), pp. 3–18; in the same collection see also "The Influence of the Liturgical Chant of the East on That of the Western Church," pp. 151–6. Recent studies have shown more parallels between the *papadike* or singers' manuals of the Byzantine tradition and Carolingian writings on music theory, among them Charles Atkinson, " 'Harmonia' and the 'Modi, quos abusive tonos dicimus,' " in *Atti del XIV Congresso della Società Internazionale di Musicologia* (Torino: EDT, 1990), pp. 485–500. See also Jørgen Raasted, "Papadike," *The New Grove,* 14:166f.

56. 19f.46–51. Compare with Lawrence Gushee, ed., Aurelian of Réome, *Musica disciplina* (Rome: American Institute of Musicology, 1975), p. 9.3f. An English version of the treatise is *Aurelian of Réome: "The Discipline of Music,"* translated by Joseph Ponte (Colorado Springs: Colorado College Music Press, 1968). The formulas used in ME and SE fit the criteria for the first Byzantine mode, that is, they descend from *a* and unfold within the fifth below. See Oliver Strunk, "Intonations and Signatures of Byzantine Music," in *Essays on Music in the Byzantine World,* p. 20. For a full treatment of these formulas in the West, see Terence Bailey, *The Intonation Formulas of Western Chant* (Toronto: Pontifical Institute of Medieval Studies, 1974).

57. For the *residui* of the daseian scale, see "The *Enchiriadis* Scale and Notation" above.

ferent from the Western ones and have a quasi-canonical status not enjoyed by the latter.

The Harmonics Tradition

Many of the concepts and terms used by ME come directly from the ancient discipline of harmonics, which was concerned with pitch and the mathematical relationships underlying pitch relations. As a Greek intellectual tradition it began with the philosopher and religious leader Pythagoras, who is said to have taught that number was the basic stuff of the universe and that the consonances of music were produced by and expressible in the arithmetic proportions underlying cosmic harmony. As a subject for detailed literary treatment, however, the harmonics tradition may be said to date from the fourth century B.C. and the *Harmonic Elements* of Aristotle's student Aristoxenus, although bits and pieces of Pythagorean music theory are scattered throughout the works of Plato, as in the *Timaeus*. Aristoxenus divides his subject into seven parts: genera, diastemata, *phthongi*, systemata, *tonoi*, modulation, and the construction of melody. All of these still find expression in the *Enchiriadis* treatises, although not necessarily in Aristoxenian terms. Absent from Aristoxenus, however, are the detailed mathematical proofs and demonstrations later employed by Ptolemy, a direct source for Boethius.[58]

Ptolemy, in his *Harmonics* (second century), offered a critique of these two received traditions—the more mystical Pythagorean and the aurally oriented, non-mathematical Aristoxenian—and gave music theory a solid mathematical basis that was confirmed by aural experience.[59] In turn, Boethius drew on Ptolemy for at least book 5 of his incompletely preserved *De institutione musica,* the first four books of which were probably based on the lost *Eisagoge musica* of Nicomachus of Gerasa.[60] Boethius's *De institutione arithmetica* and *De institutione musica* are of particular historical significance in that they represent an honest and essentially unbiased attempt to translate Greek thought into Latin.[61]

58. The lack of mathematical method is, in fact, the principal basis for Ptolemy's attack, in his *Harmonics* (second century A.D.), on the Aristoxenian tradition.

59. English translations of all major writings in Greek dealing with harmonic and acoustic theory (including those by Plato, Aristotle, Aristoxenus, Nicomachus, Ptolemy and Aristides Quintilianus) are found in the second volume of *Greek Musical Writings,* ed. Andrew Barker (Cambridge: Cambridge University Press, 1984–9).

60. See Anicius Manlius Severinus Boethius, *Fundamentals of Music,* trans. Calvin M. Bower, ed. Claude V. Palisca (New Haven and London: Yale University Press, 1989), pp. xxvi–xxix.

61. Latin accounts of Greek music theory begin with Vitruvius, *De architectura* (first cen-

The influence of Boethius on the *Enchiriadis* treatises is attested by the fact that, save one mention of Vergil in ME and one of Augustine in SE, he is the only author cited by name, and that occurs five times: in the main body of ME (43.2 and 47.39), in chapter 19 of ME (59.38), and in SE (107.165 and 132.286). He is referred to as *doctor magnificus* (44.11) and *praestantissimus auctor* (59.39). And although ME limits its obvious borrowings to the *De institutione musica* (but see below), SE also draws on his *De institutione arithmetica* and (in a more philosophical context) the *Consolatio philosophiae*.

Two direct quotations from the *De institutione musica* bring the enormous authority and prestige of the *doctor magnificus,* as transmitter of Ptolemaic principles, to bear on the problem of the eleventh, an interval used in composite organum. In chapter 11, devoted to the composite symphonies, the "natural sequence of tones" is said to be reborn at the eighth step, just as a single digit integer added to 10 becomes incorporated unchanged in the result (for example, when 2 is added to 10, the 2 is preserved in the sum 12). In the same way, intervals compounded with the octave retain the quality of the interval, whether consonant or dissonant.

After the exposition of organum at the fourth and fifth (and octave doublings thereof), chapter 16 (43.1–47.39) calls on Boethius again as expert witness to confirm that the eleventh is a consonance, stressing the virtual sameness of the two tones of an octave. Here, however, the argument is made with reference to the steps of the Greater Perfect System, in which all octaves are perfect. It is the only time in the *Enchiriadis* treatises that the names of the Greek scale steps are used. Significantly, the author stops short of using the Greater Perfect System to represent organum or octave doubling, denying at the beginning of chapter 17 the necessity of describing further such a natural and universal thing as singing in octaves. He thereby also avoids having to deal with the augmented octaves embedded in the daseian scale.

In SE the use of Boethius is quite different. Particularly notable is the extensive use of *De institutione arithmetica* for the exposition of the proportional relationships in the last portion of SE, part 2, and the bulk of part 3. However, although there are certain direct borrowings, in many cases the materials are paraphrased and intertwined with another source (especially Cassiodorus's *Institutiones*).[62]

The impact of the *De institutione musica* on the *Enchiriadis* tracts extends to other areas. The rotation principal of the daseian signs was most

---

tury B.C.). For a comprehensive survey of the Latin writers on music, see Günther Wille, *Musica romana: Die Bedeutung der Musik im Leben der Römer* (Amsterdam: Schippers, 1967).

62. See the translation, notes beginning with that to 115ff.1–39.

likely modeled on that feature of the Greek instrumental notation described by Boethius;[63] one of the signs of this notation, the so-called *tau jacens* or Ⱶ, may have inspired the choice of the basic sign for the notation, since it could be called by a more familiar name: *daseia*. In the illustrations, too, Boethius may have shown the way: examples are the letter designations A through P of figures 27 (91.*descriptio* 1) and 44 (147.*descriptio* 5).[64] Finally, certain terms are distinctly Boethian: *paginula*,[65] *bisdiapason*,[66] and the specific choice of the Greek tribal names Dorian, Phrygian, and Lydian.[67] Moreover, the famous, problematic Boethian clause *modi, quos eosdem tropos vel tonos nominant* is undoubtedly the model for the ME's phrase *modos, quos abusive tonos dicimus* (13.1f.) and SE's *tropi autem vel modi sunt, quos abusive tonos dicunt* (79.229f.), although Charles Atkinson has argued that the author of ME tried to reduce the ambiguity of the Boethian term *tonus*.[68]

A lesser but nonetheless significant influence on the harmonic theory of the *Enchiriadis* treatises is Boethius's contemporary Cassiodorus, whose presence is felt in SE in the introduction to quadrivial studies that opens the second half (at 107.160) and in the exposition of inequalities (119.60–7, 121.91–6). A third source is Censorinus's *De die natali*. From this treatise likely come one of the uses of *sescuplus* as the ratio 3:2 (21.9), the definitions of *diastema* (as interval) and *tonus* (as whole tone) in ME, chapter 9;

63. Boethius, *De inst. mus.* 4.3 (Friedlein 309ff.).

64. Compare with Boethius, *De inst. mus.* 4.14 and 4.17 (Friedlein 341.3–16 and 347.20, respectively). Phillip Spitta, "Musica enchiriadis," pp. 443–82, contains an early discussion of many aspects of the *Enchiriadis* teachings that show the influence of Boethius. Phillips *Sources*, pp. 240–72 and 345–56, is the most detailed recent treatment of this topic. Her views are summarized in "Classical and Late Latin Sources for Ninth-Century Treatises on Music," in *Music Theory and Its Sources: Antiquity and the Middle Ages*, ed. André Barbera (Notre Dame, Ind.: University of Notre Dame Press, 1990), pp. 103–8. See below for additional aspects of the treatises inspired by the writings of Boethius.

65. 36.28 and 67.117. The only documented use of this word before the *Enchiriadis* treatises is in Boethius, *De inst. mus.* 4.17 (Friedlein 343.20, 344.4, 344.7, and 347.3).

66. 134.440. This term (originally *bis diapason*) has a Latin precedent only in Boethius, *De inst. arith.* 2.48f. (Friedlein 157.19, 158.5, 159.26) and *De inst. mus.* 1.7 (Friedlein 194.26). It does not occur in ME.

67. 22.20. The choice of these three Greek tribal names (which constitute a commonplace in ancient writings on music) was probably dictated by Boethius, *De inst. mus.* 4.16 (Friedlein 343.10), which is derived from Ptolemy, *Harmonics* 2.10 (Barker, 2:336); the three names are associated with the oldest tonoi and their use by Boethius and ME continues a long tradition that includes Athenaeus, the Plutarchian treatise on music, and Dionysius of Halicarnassus. Barker, 1:213 n. 62, writes that "the thesis that ancient composers knew only these three systems seems to belong to an Aristoxenian tradition" and gives on pp. 95, 213, 295, and 299 translations of ancient sources referring to this trio. See also "The Theory of Modes" above.

68. See the translation, note to 13.1f.

the conclusion of chapter 9 (except for the integration of grammatical terminology)[69] and the opening of chapter 10 of ME; and the term *diplasion*
(39.3). Censorinus also transmits Varro's definition of music as *bene scientia
modulandi* that opens SE, although the immediate source for that, as mentioned above,[70] is more likely Augustine. Finally, vestiges of Calcidius found
in ME and SE are the idea of the diapason as the sum of the diapente and
the diatessaron, the "lambda diagram" (116.*descriptio* 1), and *sescuplus* as
the multiple 6:1 in that diagram.

The Putative Relationship to Johannes Scottus Eriugena

For the past century and a half, the name of Johannes Scottus (who also referred to himself as "Eriugena," meaning "Irish-born")[71] has been linked in
the musicological literature to the *Enchiriadis* tradition. Eriugena, the ninth-
century philosopher famous for his translations of Greek patristic writings
and for introducing into the West many post-classical Greek philosophical concepts, has been thought to have known or to have influenced the
Enchiriadis treatises, especially ME.

The original basis of this presumed connection was the discovery by
Edmond de Coussemaker[72] that the phrase *organicum melos*, which is used
in reference to polyphony in ME (38.11), also occurs in Eriugena's *De divisione naturae* or *Periphyseon* (860–7), generally regarded as the single
greatest intellectual achievement of the ninth century.[73] This coincidence led
Coussemaker to infer that Eriugena was making a specific reference to the
polyphonic practice described in ME, an inference that was accepted by
Jacques Handschin and many others,[74] but subsequently disputed by Walter
Wiora, Fritz Reckow, and Ernst Waeltner.[75] However, even they refrained

---

69. 22.26–23.32. On the grammatical element, see "Grammar and Rhetoric" above.

70. See *"Scolica enchiriadis"* above (also note 3).

71. Johannes Scottus (Eriugena), *Periphyseon (De divisione naturae), liber primus*, edited
and translated by I. P. Sheldon-Williams with Ludwig Bieler (Dublin: The Dublin Institute for
Advanced Studies, 1968), 1.

72. Edmond de Coussemaker, *Mémoire sur Hucbald et sur ses traits de musique* (Paris:
J. Techener, 1841), p. 125, and the identical *Hucbald, moine de St. Amand, et ses traits de
musique* (Douai, 1841), p. 310f. Coussemaker reiterated his position on Eriugena in his *Histoire
de l'harmonie au Moyen Âge* (Paris: Didron, 1852), p. 11.

73. The Latin text of *De divisione naturae* is in *PL*: 122:411–1022. For an English rendering,
see *Eriugena: Periphyseon (The Division of Nature)*, translated by I. P. Sheldon-Williams and
revised by John J. O'Meara (Montréal: Bellarmin, and Washington: Dumbarton Oaks, 1987).

74. Jacques Handschin, "Die Musikanschauung des Johannes Scotus," p. 323.

75. Walter Wiora, "Das vermeintliche Zeugnis des Johannes Eriugena für die Anfänge der
abendländishen Mehrstimmigkeit," *Acta musicologica* 43 (1971):33–43, documents well the
acceptance of Coussemaker's idea in the musicological literature to 1970. Wiora was the first to
question that Eriugena implied polyphony by *organicum melos*. The probable resolution of the

from suggesting that there was no connection between Eriugena and the *Enchiriadis* treatises.

Since then, Nancy Phillips has argued for a much deeper and more encompassing relationship than either Coussemaker or Handschin had envisioned. She argues that "the Neoplatonic elements in *Musica* are derived from Calcidius and Scot," that ME and SE evidence "borrowings . . . from the Christian Neoplatonism of the *corpus dionysiacum* and the writings of Scot," and that "undoubtedly there are some passages in the *Enchiriadis* treatises that are inspired by Scot."[76]

Because there are no attributed or provable direct borrowings from Eriugena's writings in the *Enchiriadis* treatises, Phillips's evidence consists only of seemingly shared terms and ideas. The most arresting case of these occur in the opening passage of ME, previously identified by William G. Waite as deriving from Calcidius.[77] However, as Phillips points out, the wording has been modified to reflect the Neoplatonic idea of procession and return,[78] a keystone of Johannes's philosophy; furthermore, Calcidius's term *dissolutio* has been replaced in ME with *resolutio,* an Eriugenean term.

Nonetheless, it can be shown that all the terms and ideas adduced as characteristic of Johannes Scottus are found earlier in the Western or Latin Neoplatonic tradition, and none of the truly distinctive features of Eastern Neoplatonism are documentable in ME or SE.[79] In fact, a likelier source than Eriugena for the Neoplatonic terms and ideas discussed is Boethius,

---

meaning of this term is found in Ernst Waeltner, *Organicum melos: Zur Musikanschauung des Iohannes Scottus (Eriugena)* (Munich: Bayerische Akademie der Wissenschaften, 1977), and in Fritz Reckow, "Organum-Begriff und frühe Mehrstimmigkeit," *Forum musicologica* 1 (Bern: Francke, 1975): 83–91 and 126.

76. Phillips *Sources,* 297, 323, and 513. The *corpus dionysiacum* refers to the body of work by Pseudo-Dionysius, thought at the time to be the same as Dionysius the Areopagite referred to in the Acts of the Apostles, 17:34; his works, translated and referred to frequently by Eriugena, came to exercise great influence in the Latin West.

77. William G. Waite, review of Guido of Arezzo, *Micrologus,* ed. Joseph Smits Van Waesberghe (Nijmegen: American Institute of Musicology, 1955), in *Journal of the American Musicological Society* 9 (1956):147f.

78. The fundamental Neoplatonic doctrine of procession and return to the One (ultimately inspired by Plato's *Parmenides*) holds that all creation is the result of first a process of successive generation ("emanation") from the One, proceeding ("processing") through the Platonic ideas to the material universe; however, the ultimate destiny of all creation is the return to union with the One. Thus, even in language the unitary letter generates successively larger constructs until an oration results; however, this oration is ultimately "dissolvable" into unitary letters.

79. Raymond Erickson, "Boethius, Eriugena, and the Neoplatonism of *Musica* and *Scolica Enchiriadis,*" in *The Legacy of Musical Humanism: Essays in Honor of Claude V. Palisca* (New York: Pendragon Press, 1992), pp. 53–78. One of the distinctive traits of Eastern Neoplatonism is "negative theology," which aspires to describe God by what He is not. Another is that the highest knowledge is not acquired by rational processes.

whose importance for the *Enchiriadis* treatises has been established above. Thus the changes to the Calcidius passage on which the opening of ME is based likely have their model in *De institutione arithmetica,* a work certainly familiar to the author of ME.[80] There Boethius not only demonstrates his acceptance of the principle of procession and return but also uses the term *resolutio.*[81] Another fact that distances the *Enchiriadis* treatises from Eriugena is the lack of any connection to Martianus Capella's *Marriage of Mercury and Philology,* the single most popular work on the liberal arts and one very closely associated with Eriugena, and yet the only major source of harmonic theory not used by the authors of ME and SE.

In sum, there is no basis for assuming a connection in either direction between the *Enchiriadis* treatises and Johannes Scottus. However, it would appear that the contribution of Boethius to the treatises is broader than previously expected—extending beyond technical terms and concepts of the harmonics tradition to include philosophical ideas derived from the *Eisagoge arithmetica* by the pagan neo-Pythagorean Nicomachus of Gerasa,[82] of which Boethius's *De institutione arithmetica* is a Latin translation.

THE *FORTUNA* OF THE *ENCHIRIADIS* TREATISES

Manuscript Transmission

In the preface to his edition, Hans Schmid lists forty-six sources, of which thirty-two contain the complete or essentially complete treatises, four are fragments of apparently once-complete texts, two contain abbreviated versions of ME, five contain the so-called *Inchiriadon,*[83] and four preserve only excerpts from ME and SE. Recently, yet another source has been discovered.[84] Of course, many MSS have been lost (including some used by Gerbert for his edition of 1784), in some cases their existence attested to only by entries in medieval library catalogues.[85] Two major studies of the MS tradition have been undertaken. Hans Schmid has published his stemma (without

---

80. Boethius, *De inst. mus.* 2.7 and 4.2 (Friedlein 232.25 and 307.26), refers the reader to his *De inst. arith.* for the mathematical information assumed in the *De inst. mus.*

81. *De inst. arith.* 2.1 (Friedlein 77.4–11).

82. *Nicomachi Geraseni Pythagorei Introductionis Arithmeticae Libri II* (in Greek), ed. Richard Hoche (Leipzig: Teubner, 1866). English translation by Martin Luther D'Ooge as Nicomachus of Gerasa, *Introduction to Arithmetic* (New York: Macmillan, 1926).

83. See "Dating: Preliminary Observations" above.

84. Fabian Lochner, "Un manuscrit de théorie musicale provenant d'Echternach: Luxembourg, B.N. MS I:21," *Scriptorium* 42 (1988):256–61.

85. Phillips *Sources,* pp. 523ff.

an explanation of how he arrived at it) in the preface to his critical edition. Nancy Phillips has not published a formal stemma but discusses in considerable detail the relationships among the MSS in chapter 2—the longest chapter—of her dissertation. The problem of the MS tradition is, in fact, an extremely complicated one,[86] since no archetype has been preserved (if one ever existed) and the oldest extant sources may be several generations after the archetype.

Phillips's analysis of the sources has led her to conclude provisionally that some melodies preserved in ME and SE were used principally in the political area of Lotharingia,[87] geographically the middle one of the three kingdoms carved out of the Carolingian empire by Charlemagne's sons at Verdun in 843; that in the tenth and early eleventh centuries ME and SE were disseminated principally in the northern part of this area, specifically, the region around Liège;[88] and that the model for manuscripts *A* (the earliest largely complete source of ME and SE) and *K* may have originated in the Cologne region east of Liège.[89] Wherever and whenever the *Enchiriadis* treatises originated and however they were disseminated, it is clear that they were among the most frequently copied and studied treatises on music: with the exception of the Boethius *De institutione arithmetica* and *De institutione musica*, the *dialogus* attributed to Odo, and the *Micrologus* of Guido of Arezzo, no medieval musical writings are preserved in a greater number of extant manuscripts.

The *Enchiriadis* Treatises in Relation to Other Pre-Guidonian Sources

In general, ME and SE appear together, in that order. But they often are accompanied by a collection of other music-theoretic writings. Some of these are directly related to the *Enchiriadis* teachings, and therefore Schmid has included them in his edition of ME and SE: the *Commemoratio brevis;* the monochord tract beginning *Super unum concavum lignum;* and a description of the modes using the terminology of the Greater Perfect System, *Ecce modorum sive tonorum.* Sometimes other independent treatises of the period also became part of the *Enchiriadis* MS tradition (among them Hucbald's *De harmonica institutione* and the anonymous *Alia musica*), but the most common companion of the *Enchiriadis* treatises is *De institutione musica*

---

86. This is indicated, for example, by the fact that Schmid and Phillips have arrived at significantly different stemmata, yet neither accounts for the same gloss to 153.612f. that is found in two MSS considered unrelated by both scholars.

87. Phillips *Sources*, p. 499.

88. Ibid.

89. Ibid., p. 413.

of Boethius. The fact that ME and SE are so transmitted has prompted Lawrence Gushee to speak of the *Enchiriadis* complex as a "superwork."[90]

The *Musica disciplina* of Aurelian of Réome,[91] accepted as the earliest Carolingian music tract, sometimes appears in manuscripts with ME and SE. Yet it obviously comes from a different intellectual environment than that which produced the *Enchiriadis* treatises. In spite of some superficial similarities—a mention of the Orpheus myth (chap. 1), borrowings from and paraphrases of Boethius and Cassiodorus (chaps. 2–4 and 6–8), descriptions of the eight modes using basic nomenclature used also ME and SE (chaps. 8 and 10–8), references to the *noannoeane* formulas (chaps. 8f. and 19), the acceptance of the eleventh as a consonance (chap. 6—from Cassiodorus), drawing the analogy between grammar and music (chap. 8)—there is little connection between Aurelian and the *Enchiriadis* treatises in substance or style. There is no precise pitch notation, no discussion of organum, and no systematic treatment of harmonic theory. Moreover, the version of the treatise normally used today was probably the result of interpolations and reworking of material over an extended period.

Much more comparable in aspiration, originality, and achievement is the work of Hucbald of St.-Amand, published by Gerbert in the eighteenth century as *De harmonica institutione*.[92] This work, like the *Enchiriadis* treatises and unlike Aurelian's, shows real understanding of Boethius and borrows many ideas from him, although they are employed somewhat differently than in ME and SE. In some respects, Hucbald's teachings show even closer adherence to Boethius than do our treatises. For example, he accepts the double-octave system, showing no awareness at all of the daseian scale.[93] In any event, brilliant as is Hucbald's synthesis of Greek, Carolingian, and Byzantine elements, the *Enchiriadis* treatises were the ones that proliferated in the tenth and eleventh centuries. Perhaps this is due in part to the fact that the *De harmonica institutione* does not deal with organum.

There are, however, some interesting parallels between the treatises. Hucbald uses (once) a notation with parallel lines like that in the *Enchiriadis*

90. Lawrence Gushee, "Questions of Genre in Medieval Treatises on Music," in *Gattungen der Musik,* ed. Wulf Arlt et al. (Bern and Munich: Francke, 1975), p. 398.

91. See note 56 above.

92. *GS* 1:104a–121a. English translation by Warren Babb in *Hucbald, Guido, and John,* pp. 13–44.

93. Hucbald does use the daseia (which name he uses) as the sign for proslambanomenos (*GS* 1:120; Babb translation, fig. 16 on p. 38). But this is clearly derived from Boethius, not the *Enchiriadis* teachings, despite some changes to, or misunderstandings about, the Boethian letter notation by Hucbald. Boethius describes the Greek notation in *De inst. mus.* 4.15–17 (Friedlein 341–8 and two diagrams to p. 343 that are in the appendix).

tracts,[94] and he speaks of the *socialitas* of pitches a fifth above.[95] He utilizes in his treatment of the modes successive examples of essentially the same melody with the texts "Alleluia" and "Nonenoeane," respectively; these have parallels in ME and SE, respectively.[96] Moreover, one of Hucbald's two scales is built out of tone-semitone-tone tetrachords.[97] Finally, both Hucbald and SE share the interesting harmonic division that results in a C-major scale, as well as a division of the traditional double octave on A.[98]

The complex of tracts called *Alia musica,* which applies the ethnic names of the Ptolemaic-Boethian tonoi or keys to the church modes and which relates the church modes to species of octave, is a work that is part of the *Enchiriadis* MS tradition yet has little substantive connection to it. Jacques Chailley has proposed that all three parts of *Alia musica,* as well as Hucbald's treatise, are to be dated in the late ninth century but *before* ME, which he posited to have been written around 895 in the region of St.-Amand, near Valenciennes.[99] Phillips, on the other hand, thinks that *Alia musica* as presently known dates from the late tenth century but includes modifications of some material dating as far back as the ninth century.[100] The point to emphasize is that *Alia musica,* unlike ME, SE, and Hucbald, defines the church modes in terms of octave species, which, according to Phillips's hypothesis, would have no relevance until about the eleventh century, when theory and chant melodies both reflected octave-based thinking. Supporting her thesis is the fact that ME does not take up species at all, whereas SE discusses species of fourth and fifth but, significantly, not octave species.

Guido and the *Enchiriadis* Tradition

The majority of the extant *Enchiriadis* manuscripts were copied in the late tenth and eleventh centuries. Thus the treatises had widespread currency

94. *GS* 1:109b (Babb translation, p. 23, fig. 4).

95. *GS* 1:119b (Babb translation: "relationship," p. 39).

96. For Hucbald, see *GS* 1:117b–118a (Babb translation 36f., figs. 25 and 26); for ME and SE, respectively, see 14.*descriptio* 1 (fig. 8.1) and 78.*descriptio* 17 (fig. 17).

97. *GS* 1:110ab (Babb translation, p. 24, fig. 5). Even though it is possible that there is a common model for the tone-semitone-tone tetrachord in Byzantine practice, Hucbald and the *Enchiriadis* authors nonetheless construct fundamentally different scales as the basis of their modal theories. The compass of the *Enchiriadis* scale is not a double octave as are both of Hucbald's, and the lowest note in Hucbald's scale is A, which precludes the possibility of G as the lower boundary of the protus mode as implied in ME (9.9f. and 9.1–5) and SE (85.365–71).

98. For Hucbald, see *GS* I:110b–111a (Babb translation, p. 25, and fig. 6 on p. 24); for SE, 145.*descriptio* 4 (fig. 43) and 147.*descriptio* 5 (fig. 44). See also "Demonstrations" above.

99. Jacques Chailley, *Alia musica* (Paris: Institut de Musicologie de l'Université de Paris, 1964), pp. 59f.

100. Phillips *Sources,* p. 231 n. 48.

in the period just before the influence of Guido d'Arezzo swept Europe. This is reflected in part by the remarks of Guido himself, whose *Micrologus* shows familiarity with the *Enchiriadis* treatises and sometimes contrasts their teachings with his own.[101] Some points of contact in his modal theory, for example, are phrases like "modes or tropes, which are improperly called 'tones'" (*Micrologus,* chapter 10; Schmid 13.1f. and 79.229f.); errors in singing such as are covered in SE (*Micrologus,* chapter 7; Schmid 65.92–72.151); and a borrowed (if more developed) concept of defining the quality of an individual step by the intervals surrounding it,[102] which results in modal identity not only at the fifth but also at the fourth.[103] Thus, Guido's *affinalis* has a likeness to SE's *socialis* and *compar* for the fifth degree (82.318 and 73.159, respectively), and *compar* possibly for the fourth degree as well (82.320).

Guido reflects the view of most of the organum tracts between the *Enchiriadis* treatises and his own that the fourth is the primary interval of organum (*Micrologus,* chap. 18). The seeds of this may be in ME, which treats the perfect consonances in the order diatessaron, diapente, and octave, and introduces organum at the fourth before organum at the fifth, even though the former is more complicated and requires two later chapters for a full explanation. Hence, it would appear that some priority is assigned to organum at the fourth in ME.[104] Regardless of ME's intent, the fourth is the only, the preferred, or the "natural" interval of organum in theoretical expositions between the *Enchiriadis* treatises and Guido; these include the first Bamberg dialogue, the Schlettstadt tract, the Cologne treatise, and the *De organo* appended to the *Inchiriadon.* The second Bamberg dialogue, exceptionally, gives the diatessaron and diapente equal standing as organal intervals.[105]

For Guido, however, only organum at the fourth (with neither, one, or both voices doubled at the octave above) is the traditional way, a style he calls "hard" (*durus; Micrologus,* chap. 18). His own "soft" (*mollis*) style permits simultaneities of unison, whole tone, major and minor thirds, and

---

101. Guido of Arezzo, *Micrologus;* Babb translation, pp. 57–83.

102. Guido, *Micrologus,* chap. 7, refers to such an interval complex as a *modus vocum.*

103. Thus, according to Guido, *Micrologus,* chaps. 8 and 9, D, A and G may all be called protus (if the melodic ascent from the last involves B♭).

104. However, in SE the consonances are treated in descending order of consonance, and multi-voice singing is correspondingly treated in the order octave doubling, organum at the fifth, and organum at the fourth.

105. These tracts are edited, with German translation, in Ernst Waeltner, *Die Lehre von Organum bis zur Mitte des 11. Jahrhunderts* (Tutzing: Hans Schneider, 1975). Moreover, all except the Schlettstadt tract are also edited by Schmid in the appendix to his edition of *Musica* and *Scolica enchiriadis.*

perfect fourth; the voices come together at the ends of phrases, a procedure foreshadowed in the special law regulating organum at the fourth in the *Enchiriadis* treatises (ME, chap. 18, and SE, 102f.86–91).

The Reichenau School

Later in the eleventh century, at the abbey of Reichenau, the abbot Berno and his brilliant protégé Hermann (called "Contractus" because of a crippling infirmity) developed methods of modal definition in terms of species of fourth and fifth. Although they are not dealing with the theory and practices of the ninth century and do not discuss polyphony, both authors reveal thorough familiarity with the *Enchiriadis* teachings.

In Berno's *Prologus in tonarium*, this is seen mainly in numerous common terms and formulations that are found, sometimes uniquely, in ME or SE, especially the latter. His concern is for the *peritus cantor* (GS 2:74a, 76b, 78a; Schmid 57.4, 60f.10f.), who should be more than just a singer. Berno also speaks of eight modes "which we wrongly call tones" (GS 2:68a), of which four are classed as *authenticus, authentus,* or *magister,* and four *plagis, lateralis,* or *subiugalis.* He also adopts (GS 2:68b–69a) the *magister/discipulus* dichotomy of Aurelian (*Musica disciplina,* chapter 8), whose treatise is part of the *Enchiriadis* "superwork." He incorporates the ubiquitous Vergilian phrase *septem vocum discrimen* (GS 2:69a; Schmid 33.27f.), refers to chants that end on non-standard finals as *irregularis* and *illegitimus* (GS 2:69a), and describes phrase structures using the grammatico-rhetorical terms first applied to music by the *Enchiriadis* authors: *colon, comma, membrum, distinctio* (GS 2:70b, 75a; Schmid 22.23ff., 82f.327–33, 85.371–3).

Particularly striking is a passage where Berno describes how "in antiquity" "they declared the descent of many chants to be indistinguishable between authentics and subordinates," a point of view transmitted only by ME and SE (GS 2:71b; Schmid 8.4, 85.365–71). The upper limit of the authentic mode is also described in terms that have their closest parallels in SE:

Berno of Reichenau: Animadvertendum nunc est: cum omnis authenticus a suo finali incipiens licenter in nonum sonum ascendat; non quod semper id eveniat, sed quod haec eius scandendi fit potestas. (GS 2:72a)
Now it must be noticed that every authentic mode, beginning from its final, may ascend to the ninth tone. This does not always happen, but such is the potential of its ascent.

SE: A finali sono aequalis potestas est minori tono in superiora atque inferiora.... Non quod semper id eveniat, sed quod haec spacii eius sit potestas. . . . Maior autem sistematis duplum habet spatium . . . usque in nonum sonum. (85.365–71)

> In a plagal mode the potential range [*potestas*] from the final is equal above and
> below. . . . This does not always happen, but this is its potential range. . . . An
> authentic mode has . . . a range . . . up to the ninth tone [above the final].

Another interesting pair of passages is the following:

> Berno of Reichenau: Fit etiam miro quodam modo, ut finales non solum in quintis,
> ut diximus, regionibus suos habeant sociales, verum etiam in quartis superioribus
> locis sibi inveniant compares: ut quemadmodum membra cantionum, quae sunt
> cola & commata, in finalibus & in quintis locis, ita per arsin & thesin consistant
> saepius in quartis. Amplius autem, quod omnis tropus, sive ille authenticus fit
> sive plagis, si quarto a finali loco diligentius intueatur, mira ac divina quaedam
> concordia inveniatur. Ita ut si quis cantus a finali in quartum locum transponatur,
> legitime videatur sub eodem modo vel tono currere, et in eodem velut in finali
> regulariter desinere. (GS 2:75a)
>
> In a certain wonderful way, just as the finals have their associated tones [*sociales*]
> at the fifth as we have said, so too they find compeers at the fourth above.[106] In
> this way, through *arsis* and *thesis,* the phrases of songs, which are *cola* and *com-
> mata,* end on the finals and at the fifth, [and] more often at the fourth. Further,
> however, because every mode, whether authentic or plagal, is treated more care-
> fully if at the fourth from the final, it is found to have a certain marvelous and
> divine concord. Thus, if any chant is transposed from the final to the fourth, it
> runs legitimately in the same mode or tone and ends, according to rule, on the
> same [fourth step], as if it were the final.

> SE: Additur hoc tamen, quod sonus idem finalis et sociales sui frequentiores in
> commatum vel colarum fine versantur. Sociales autem suos quisque sonus non
> solum quintis habet regionibus, sed et quartis locis alios sibi quaerit compares,
> qui tertiae simphoniae locus est. Itaque in particulis, quae membra sunt cantionis,
> pene semper solo vel commata has in levando aut in ponendo sonorum socialitates
> putunt, et in eas vel arsis quaerit attingere vel thesis. (82.319–23)
>
> It must be added, however, that the final tone and its more usual associated tones
> are found at the ends of commas or colons. Moreover, each tone not only has
> associated tones [*sociales*] at the fifth, but it also seeks those others comparable
> to itself at the fourth, which is the place of the third symphony. So in phrases that
> are members of a song, the colons or commas, ascending or descending, nearly
> always seek out these tones associated with the final, and the melody, whether
> ascending or descending, seeks to reach them.

Although Berno claims more for melodies transposed at the interval of the
fourth than does SE, the many similarities in terminology seem hardly a
matter of chance.

Toward the end of the *Prologus* (GS 2:77ab), Berno speaks of dura-

---

106. Regarding "compeers" see the note to 73.159.

tional aspects of chant performance, of how certain tones are appropriately lengthened or shortened, the tempo increased or decreased. He explains that *numerositas* or rhythm shares with pitch a common basis in proportionality: as in metrics a verse is constructed by a certain measure of feet, so is a chant composed of an apt and harmonious, thus necessarily proportional, coupling of short and long tones. This recalls the end of part 1 of SE (86.384–89.429).

In Hermanus Contractus there are still reminiscences of the *Enchiriadis* treatises, although the approach is very different.[107] He posits four tetrachords of tone-semitone-tone form, beginning on the low A and with an added step at the top. The names of these tetrachords correspond to those of the daseian scale. But the pitches do not, since the tetrachords (of which the graves is ranked principal) are arranged in two conjunct pairs separated by a whole-tone of disjunction (as in the Greater Perfect System). Hermann specifically criticizes the arrangement of the daseian scale as "against nature"; by his time it probably was in fact unsuitable for chant melodies, which had undergone changes over the preceding two centuries. He complains further that, in the daseian scale, steps eight steps apart do not even have the same name.

The *Quaestiones in musica*

Finally, there is the treatise on chant known as the *Quaestiones in musica*,[108] probably from the late eleventh or early twelfth century, which is studded with quotations or reworkings of passages from a variety of unattributed sources, including Boethius, Berno, Guido, Aribo, and the *Enchiriadis* treatises. The extent of the borrowings from ME and especially SE is too great to be detailed here, but Rudolf Steglich's edition provides easy comparison by laying out the *Quaestiones* and its source texts in parallel columns. It can be said, however, that a significant portion of the second half of SE, from 106.143 through 144.510, the heart of the mathematical teachings of SE, is found in the *Quaestiones*.

The *Enchiriadis* Treatises in Modern Times

The modern history of the study of the *Enchiriadis* treatises begins with their publication in 1784 (as writings of Hucbald) in Martin Gerbert's *Scriptores ecclesiastici de musica*.[109] But even before that they were discussed by

---

107. Hermanus Contractus, *Musica*, translated by Leonard Ellinwood (Rochester: Eastman School of Music, 1936), contains both an edition of the Latin text and English translation.

108. Edited with commentary by Rudolf Steglich, *Die Quaestiones in musica* (Leipzig: Breitkopf und Härtel, 1911).

109. ME and SE are found in GS 1:152–73 and 173–212, respectively.

Charles Burney,[110] and at the turn of the century Forkel gave considerable space to them.[111] In the nineteenth century important strides were made by Hans Müller (who proved that the author of the *Enchiriadis* treatises was not Hucbald),[112] Phillip Spitta (who discerned many of the important borrowings of the *Enchiriadis* authors from Boethius),[113] and Raymund Schlecht (who translated both treatises into German).[114] Yet it is only in the 1980s that a reliable critical text of the treatises, by Hans Schmid, became available,[115] aiding the comprehensive study of Phillips and making this English translation possible.

Conclusion

Historians refer to the "Carolingian Renaissance" of the ninth century yet often argue that its artistic contribution to Western civilization was minimal, producing virtually no lasting masterpieces of painting, architecture, or poetry. Nonetheless, the music historian can point to many innovative achievements in the realm of musical art that had lasting impact: the substantial enlargement of the repertoire through new melodies and even new categories of chant (such as trope and sequence), music notation, the theory of the modes, and rules for singing polyphony. But these were not generated in a vacuum: they arose naturally in a culture in which the legacy of the ancient past was being reinterpreted for use in contemporary life, producing results that were genuinely Western, European, *abendländisch*. No documents better exemplify this spirit and achievement than the *Enchiriadis* treatises.

110. Charles Burney, *A General History of Music* (London, 1776–89; repr. New York: Dover Publications, 1957) 1:489–91.

111. Johann Nikolaus Forkel, *Allgemeine Geschichte der Musik* (Leipzig, 1788–1801; repr. Graz: Akademische Druck- und Verlagsanstalt, 1967) 2:304–13.

112. *Hucbalds echte und unechte Schriften über Musik* (Leipzig: Teubner, 1884). Gerbert had indicated that Hucbald was the author of the *Enchiriadis* treatises.

113. Spitta, "Die *Musica enchiriadis* und ihr Zeitalter."

114. "Die *Musica enchiriadis* von Hucbald," *Monatshefte für Musikgeschichte* 6 (1874): 163–91; 7 (1875):1–30, 33–45, 50–61, 65–93; and 8 (1876):89–101.

115. Whereas the critical texts of ME and SE themselves are reliable, the critical apparatus of the Schmid edition is not always so. See Phillips's review, *Journal of the American Musicological Society* 36 (1983):129–43.

[Musica enchiriadis]

1. HERE BEGINS THE MUSIC HANDBOOK[1]

[3] Just as the elementary and indivisible constituents[2] of speech (*vox articulata*) are letters, from which syllables are put together, and these in turn make up verbs and nouns, and from them is composed the fabric of a complete discourse, so the roots of song (*vox canora*) are *phthongi*, which are called *soni* in Latin.[3] The content of all music is ultimately reducible to them.

From the coupling of tones (*soni*) come intervals (*diastemata*); from intervals, in turn, grow systems (*systemata*).[4] Tones, however, are the primal elements of song.[5] Not all sounds (*soni*) are called tones (*ptongi*) [but] only

1. 3, title *INCIPIT LIBER ENCHIRIADIS DE MUSICA*. ME is without title in fifteen manuscripts (including the tenth-century *A*, the most important early source) and, in fact, all chapter titles in ME are later additions. See introduction, "The Titles." Bracketed numbers refer to pages in Schmid's edition.

2. 3.1 (*partes*). The obvious translation of *partes* as "parts" has been avoided to preclude confusion with grammatical "parts of speech."

3. 3.3–4 (*ptongi, qui Latine dicuntur soni*). In this translation, both *p[h]t[h]ongus* and *sonus* (unless otherwise indicated) will be rendered as "tone" when referring to a discrete musical sound, whereas *vox,* when used in this sense, will be translated "pitch." *Tonus,* which means either "mode" or "whole tone" in the *Enchiriadis* treatises, is therefore not a synonym for *phthongus, sonus,* or *vox.* On *tonus,* see the note to 4.18.

4. 3.5–6. *Diastema* and *systema,* terms of Greek harmonic theory used in the Calcidius grammar/music analogy, are not defined until chap. 9 (22f.26–32).

5. 3.1–7. The opening of ME to this point is a reworking of 1.44 of Calcidius's commentary on Plato's *Timaeus* (Waszink 92.10–9). See also introduction, "The Putative Relationship to Johannes Scottus Eriugena."

those which, by virtue of being at proper distances from each other, are apt for melody. Thus a series of them is joined together, ascending and descending in a natural way, so that they follow one another [4], always in similarly constituted groups of four.[6] The four individual members of these groups are dissimilar from each other in their mutual diversity such that not only do they differ in highness and lowness, but [also] in this very highness and lowness each has the special quality of its own nature determined by fixed mutual distances above and below the individual tones. For the sake of illustration, figure 1.1 gives in order their note-forms (*notae*).

Figure 1.1

The first and lowest is that which is called *protus* or *archous* in Greek. The second, *deuterus,* is a whole tone from protus.[7] The third, *tritus,* is a semitone from deuterus. The fourth, *tetrardus,* is a whole tone from tritus. By a continuous multiplication of these tones, an unlimited series is made as they proceed in similarly constituted groups of four until they run out ascending or descending, [5] as in figure 1.2. This little illustration shows

Figure 1.2

6. 4.10 (*quattuor et quattuor eiusdem conditionis*). The concept of *conditio* as used in ME and SE encompasses not only the ordinal position of tones within a tetrachord but also the intervallic, i.e., modal, relationships among them.

7. 4.18 (*tono*). Concerning the translation of *tonus* in ME and SE: (1) when signifying the interval *tonus,* it will be translated as "whole tone," as here; (2) when signifying an ecclesiastical chant mode, it will be rendered as "mode," the only exception being at 13.1f., where the context demands it be given as the cognate "tone" (see also the note to 13.1f.); (3) *tonus* never appears in ME and SE as a synonym for *phthongus, vox,* or *sonus.*

that you may extend the tones up or down in a series until the voice gives out; the succession of these tetrachords will not cease. From the character (*virtus*) of these four tones also comes the character (*potestas*)[8] of the eight modes (*modi*), as will be described later in the appropriate place. Every harmonious assemblage [of the tones] is unified by their mutual diversity.

Because, as has been said, the multiplication of these tones proceeds unendingly, the theory of this discipline selects for itself a fixed number out of such confusing prolixity, limiting consideration to eighteen tones. Among these [groups of four] the first and lowest make up the tetrachord of the *graves* tones. Next to this is the tetrachord of the *finales*. After them comes the tetrachord of the *superiores*. Next follows that of the *excellentes*. At the end, two tones remain. Figure 1.3 illustrates these things.

Figure 1.3

2. CONCERNING THE SYMBOLS FOR THE TONES AND WHY THERE ARE EIGHTEEN

[6] Since, as has been said, nature has ordained similarly constituted groups of four, so too are the note-forms for them almost the same. The different tetrachords are represented merely by turning the symbols in various ways.

The [symbol for the] first finalis or *terminalis* [tone] is a slanted daseia⊦ with an S at the top, thus *ℱ*; that for the second finalis has a turned C at the top, thus *ℱ*; the third finalis is a simple, but slanted, iota, thus *ʃ*; the fourth finalis has a half C on the top, thus *ℱ*; the graves [symbols] are the finales in reverse, thus ϡ ϡ Ν ϡ; the superiores [symbols] are the finales fallen on their heads, thus ↲ ↲ Ц ↲; the excellentes [symbols] are the graves fallen on their heads, thus ↳ ↳ ⨕ ↳.

---

8. 5.34–7 (*quattuor sonorum virtus octo modorum potestam creat*). *Virtus* and *potestas*—along with *vis, proprietas*, and *qualitas*—are essentially synonymous words denoting innate nature, quality, potency, or character. These terms are never precisely defined or differentiated in ME and SE, nor are they used extensively in earlier Latin writings in reference to musical elements or constructs. In this translation, the individual words are rendered (unless otherwise noted) as follows: *vis:* "nature"; *virtus* and *potestas:* "character"; *proprietas:* "properties"; *qualitas:* "quality."

The exception is the tritus, which in the graves has as the symbol a slanted N: /\/; in the superiores a reversed and slanted N: /; ; and in the excellentes the iota pierced through: /. The two [7] remaining tones have the signs of protus and deuterus lying on their sides: ⌐³   ⌐². There are eighteen in all, which means that the individual tones[9] attain their farthest symphony,[10] namely, the fifteenth tone, as will be explained later.[11] There are also many other signs invented in former times for many tones,[12] but we must begin with the easier ones.

3. WHY THE TETRACHORD OF THE FINALS IS SO CALLED, AND OTHER MATTERS

The terminal tones or finals are so called because every melody must end on one of these four [tones]. Indeed, a melody in the first mode and its plagal (*subiugalis*) is ruled and ended by the archous tone ⨍[D]. The second mode with its plagal is ruled and ended by the deuterus tone ⨍[E]. The third and its plagal [8] is ruled and ended by the tritus tone /[F]. The fourth with its plagal is ruled and ended by the tetrardus tone ⨍[G]. Any greater (*maior*) mode is called authentic (*autentus*); any lesser (*minor*) is called plagal (*plagis*).

4. WHY ONLY ONE TETRACHORD IS UNDER THE FINALS BUT TWO ARE ABOVE

The finals or terminal tones have under them one tetrachord, which is called [the tetrachord] of the graves [tones]; however, there are two [tetrachords] above them, that is, those of the superiores and the excellentes, with two tones left over. And so a monophonic and properly made chant[13] does

---

9. 7.14 (*singuli*). *Singuli* must refer to the four tones protus, deuterus, etc., which, in their lowest positions only, do have a counterpart two octaves higher. This is also the sense of the eleventh-century gloss at this point in N.

10. 7.14 (*extremam symphoniam*). This is the first use in ME of *symphonia*, the term for a perfect consonance. *Symphonia* is defined in chap. 10 (23.5f.) and does not necessarily imply simultaneity.

11. 7.15 (*unde post dicetur*). The reference is to chapter 11.

12. 7.16. Undoubtedly a reference to the ancient notations described in Boethius, *De inst. mus.* 4.3 and 4.4 (Friedlein, 308–14). A gloss in P specifically cites Boethius.

13. 8.3. *Simplex et legitimus cantus* (a similar phrase is also found in SE at 86.379) is glossed in P with *simplex cantus dicitur sine organo, et legitimus, qui mensuram sibi inditam non excedit* ("A 'simple' melody is defined as one without organum, a 'proper' melody one which does not exceed the range appointed to it"). Furthermore, N glosses *legitimus* with *qui non transit suum terminum ascendendo et descendendo* ("which does not exceed its limit in ascending or descending"). However, both manuscripts are eleventh-century sources.

not descend below the fifth tone from its final: specifically, [a chant] in the first and second modes [descends] from ƒ⃔ [D] *archous* or *protus finalis* down to the same in the graves ⅄ [GG]; one in the third and fourth from ƒ⃕ [E] *deuterus finalis* down to the same gravis tone Ɉ [A]; one in the fifth and sixth from ∫ [F] *tritus finalis* down to the same [9] gravis tone ⋀ [Bb]; and one in the seventh and eighth from ƒ⃔ [G] *tetrardus finalis* down to the same gravis tone ⅄ [C]. However, it is permitted to ascend from any final up to the third tone of the same name, that is, as far as the *excellentes*.[14]

5. HOW AUTHENTIC AND LESSER MODES DIFFER

Any authentic mode and that which is under it [i.e., its plagal] may be governed by and end on the same tone, whence they also are considered to be one and the same mode. They differ, however, in this: the range ascending is less in the plagal modes, and no plagal mode ascends beyond the fifth tone from its final, except in rare instances. [10]

6. CONCERNING THE PROPERTIES OF THE TONES AND HOW MANY POSITIONS FROM ONE ANOTHER TONES OF THE SAME QUALITY MAY BE

Whoever delights in pursuing these things may consider to what extent he may learn to distinguish the special nature (*vis*) of any tone (*sonus*)—hence, how to identify quickly, among tones mixed together, any tone (*phthongus*), whether low or high. In this way the distance between any tone and another may easily be reckoned by both character and notation. Every musical tone has a tone of identical quality a fifth away on either side, tones that share another quality a third away on either side, and whatever [quality] a tone has at the second on one side will be at the fourth on the other.

Something must also be offered those less practiced in these things so they may learn either to differentiate the respective qualities of the tones in any known melody or to decipher an unknown melody from the quality and ordering of the tones known through their signs. And in this process of discovery it helps not a little [11] to sing in order the Greek names of the signs through the neighboring tones as in figure 6.1.[15]

14. 9.9–10 (*At vero in acumine . . . usque in excellentes*). This rule regarding the upper limit (here given as the ninth above the final) actually applies only to the authentic modes, since the upper limit for plagal modes is defined otherwise in chap. 5 immediately following.

15. 11.*descriptio* (fig. 6.1). The intended execution of these melodic formulas, described imprecisely in the opening of chap. 7 (11.1–4 and 12.*descriptio* [fig. 7.1]) is possibly indicated in

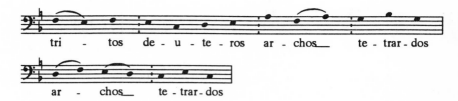

Figure 6.1

7. SHORT DESCRIPTIONS OF THE PROPERTIES OF THE TONES FOR PURPOSES OF PRACTICING

When someone sings each tone in this fashion using its proper name, one easily perceives in the singing which of the tones it is. By way of example, a melody (*carmen*) is represented in figure 7.1,[16] wherein the musical note-forms written above the syllables are sung to the names given above these symbols. [12] [13] If by chance the identity of any tone is strongly doubted, then the tones in order are tested for semitones, which, it is known, always separate deuterus from tritus. Soon it will be clear which tone is involved, since practice makes notating or singing tones as easy as writing and reading letters. These things are said to help beginners with their study.

SE, part 3, 153f.*descriptiones* 8a–b (figs. 47a–b). Both SE and the *Inchiriadon* (191.125f.) have larger sets of examples, the ascending and descending sequences of which make logical sense, whereas the order of examples in ME (fig. 6.1) is puzzling. That the series begins with tritus suggests an incomplete set of examples. In fig. 6.1 and subsequent transcriptions, melodies in daseian notation will be indicated by a "mixed key signature" that corresponds to the relevant portion of the daseian pitch-set.

    16. 12.*descriptio* (fig. 7.1). In this transcribed version of the illustration, the daseian "note-forms written above the syllables" have been replaced by noteheads on a staff. The illustration as given by Schmid presumes to correct the confusing and error-ridden form of the earliest sources (including *A*), which probably derive from the miscopying of a model that had to be read by rotating the exemplar ninety degrees. Cf. Nancy Phillips and Michel Huglo, "The Versus *Rex caeli*: Another Look at the So-Called Archaic Sequence," *Journal of the Plainsong and Medieval Music Society* 5 (1982):39–41, which argues against the traditional notion that *Rex caeli* is a sequence. Peter Dronke, "Types of Poetic Art in Tropes," *Münchener Beiträge zur Mediavistik und Renaissance-Forschung* 36 (1985):1f. n. 2, does not accept this, however, and also criticizes Schmid's reordering of the text phrases. *Rex caeli* appears again in chaps. 17 and 18 (49.*descriptio* and 51.*descriptio* [figs. 17.1 and 18.1]), but the phrases *squalidique soli* and *maris undisoni* are exchanged in 49.*descriptio* (fig. 17.1), as in the manuscript sources. *Rex caeli* is also used for illustration—with daseian signs but without linear diagrams—in the *Inchiriadon* (188.33f.) and, uniquely with complete text, following the so-called second Bamberg dialogue on organum (218f.), interpolated within ME in *H*. Phillips, in her review of Schmid, 136, calls this last the "best edition [of *Rex caeli*] to date," whereas Dronke regards it as "faulty."

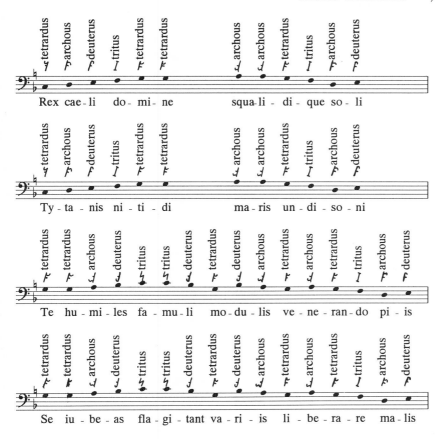

Rex cae-li do-mi-ne   squa-li - di - que so-li

Ty - ta - nis ni - ti - di   ma - ris un - di - so - ni

Te hu - mi - les fa - mu - li   mo - du - lis ve - ne - ran-do pi - is

Se iu - be - as fla - gi - tant va - ri - is   li - be - ra - re ma - lis

Figure 7.1

8. HOW THE MODES ARE PRODUCED FROM THE NATURE OF THE FOUR TONES

It must now be demonstrated how the nature of the four tones regulates the modes, which we improperly call "tones,"[17] and how such an arrange-

17. 13.1–2 (*modos, quos abusive tonos dicimus*). Here is the only instance in this translation where *tonus* is rendered as "tone," as synonym for an ecclesiastical melodic "mode" (see note to 4.18f.). *Tonus* (and never *modus*) had been the standard way to refer to the eight modes since the eighth century (for example, in the tonaries and in Aurelian's treatise). Therefore, it is somewhat surprising to read that this term, which also appears later in the chapter (19.46f.), is incorrect. Atkinson, "*Harmonia* and the *Modi, quos abusive tonos dicimus*," proposes that ME's critique of then standard terminology was influenced by Boethius, who had tried to reduce the ambiguity inherent in the Greek term τόνος and hence in its Latin cognate *tonus*. (Cf. Boethius, *De inst. mus.* 4.15 [Friedlein 341.19–21]: *modi quos eosdem tropos vel tonos*

ment is made. For example, let some "strings" (*chordae*), as it were, be extended straight out [14] from the individual symbols for the tones positioned in order. Moreover, let the lines (*chordae*) stand for the pitches these symbols signify. On these lines any melody may be represented, as in figure 8.1.[18]

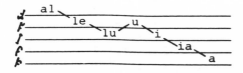

Figure 8.1

To confirm, both by ear and eye, what is being said, let us make another little illustration using the same melody. After the lines have been drawn from side to side, a four-fold series is successively written out between the lines, such that each series may be distinguished by its own appearance (*color*).[19] Indeed, the series of the first melody begins from the tone ⊿ [a] and ends on the tone Ϝ [D]. The second starts from the tone ⌡ [b] and finishes on the tone Ϝ [E]. The third begins from the tone Ϥ [c] [15] and concludes on

---

nominant, "the modes that are also called tropes or tones.") Atkinson points out that, once *tonus* and *modus* are defined in ME, chap. 9, as a whole tone and mode, respectively, ME holds to this distinction for the rest of the treatise. This is not true, however, for SE, in which *tonus* for "mode" is similarly criticized (79.229f.: *Tropi autem vel modi sunt, quos abusive tonos dicunt*). Yet *tonus* continues to be used, alongside *modus* and *tropus*, for "mode" from 77.215 (in part 1) to 105.139 (in part 2).

18. 14.*descriptio* 1 (fig. 8.1). In all the original diagrams of this type rendered in Schmid's edition, the lines underneath the syllables (but not the spaces between them) represent the tones of the melody. The given example is one of a family of similarly formed melodies found in tonaries and theoretical tracts as intonations for first mode chants. See Bailey, *Intonation Formulas*, p. 48, for a summary of these first-mode formulas. See also Schmid 78.*descriptio* 17 [SE, fig. 17], which has a slightly different melody with text *Noannoeane* in various modal transpositions, a treatment similar to 15.*descriptio* 2 [fig. 8.2].

19. 14.10 (*suo proprio colore*). The earliest manuscripts apparently used different colors for different lines, but the tradition was not consistently followed. See Phillips *Sources*, p. 216. Schmid's critical apparatus does not indicate the use of colors in either 14.*descriptio* 1 or 15.*descriptio* 2 (figs. 8.1 and 8.2), but see note to 36.21–3.

the tone ⟨ [F]. The fourth commences from the tone ⟨ [d] and stops on the tone ⟨ [G]. Hence [see figure 8.2].

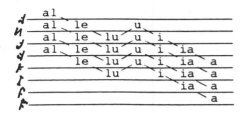

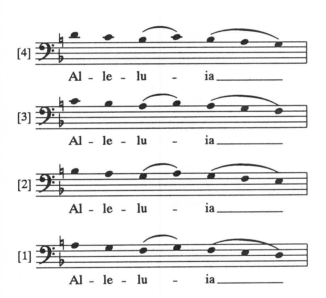

Figure 8.2

These four individual examples, while they are separated only by a semi-tone or whole tone—that is, by a harmonic interval—are changed (*transponere*) by that alone from one type [of mode] to another. When you sing the first version, you will be able to discern that the nature of the first tone ⟨ produces the character (*virtus*) of the first mode, which is called *protus authenticus*. When you sing the second, you will perceive that the deuterus mode is governed by the deuterus tone ⟨. Taking the third, you will see that the character (*potestas*) of the tritus mode similarly resides in the tritus tone ⟨. When you have sung the fourth, you will understand that the category (*genus*) of the tetrardus mode proceeds from the tetrardus tone ⟨ .

[16] Therefore, any melodies whatsoever of the first mode and its plagal can be related to the first melody (*modulatio*)—similarly those of the second, of the third, and of the fourth, following the examples of individual modes below. I have attempted to illustrate these things in two ways for clearer understanding, both linearly, as with strings, and also by attaching symbols to the individual syllables. A melody in the principal protus mode and its plagal follows [figure 8.3].[20]

Figure 8.3

Al⌡le𝄒lu ∫𝄒∫ ia𝄒𝄒. Lau ∫ da𝄒 ⌡te𝄒 Do𝄒 mi∫ num 𝄒 de ∫𝄒 coe 𝄒lis𝄒.

Cae ∫ li 𝄒 cae𝄒lo ∫ rum 𝄒 lau𝄒⅂ da𝄒te 𝄒∫ De𝄒um𝄒.

[17] A melody in the principal deuterus mode and its plagal [fig. 8.4]:

Figure 8.4

---

20. 16.30. The alleluia melodies for figs. 8.3–6 have already been given in 15.*descriptio* 2 (fig. 8.2).

Al ♩ le ♩ lu ⌐ ♩ ⌐ ia ʃ ⌐.

Con ⌐ fi ♩ te ⅂ bor ♩⌐ Do ♩ mi ♩ no ⌐ ni ♩ mis ♩ in ⌐ o ⌐ ʃ re ⌐ me ⌐ o ⌐.

Lau ⌐ da ⌐ ʃ bo ⌐ De ⌐ um ʃ me ⌐ ♩ um ⌐ in ʃ vi ⌐ ta ⌐ ʃ me ⌐ a ⌐.

[18] A melody in the principal tritus mode and its plagal [figure 8.5]:

Figure 8.5

Al ⅂ le ♩ lu ♩♩ ♩ ia ⌐ ʃ.

In ⅂ tel ⅂ le ⅂ ♩ ge ♩ cla ♩ mo ♩ rem ♩ me ♩ um ⌐ Do ♩ mi ⌐ ne ʃ.

Mi ʃ se ⌐ re ♩ re ⌐ ʃ me ⌐ ♩ i ⌐ De ʃ us ʃ.

A melody in the principal tetrardus mode and its plagal [19] [figure 8.6]:

Figure 8.6

Al ♩ le ⅂ lu ♩ ⅂ ♩ ia ♩ ⌐.

Sit ♩ ♩ no ♩ men ⅂ Do ♩ ⌐ mi ♩ ni ⅂ be ⅂ ♩ ne ♩ dic ♩ ⅂ tum ♩ in ♩ sae ⌐ cu ⌐ la ⌐.

In *ʼʃ* ae *♩* ter *ʼʃ* num *♩* et *ꜰ ʃ* in *ꜰ* sae *♩ ♩* cu *♩* lum *♩* sae *♩ ꜰ* cu *ʃ ꜰ* li *ꜰ.*

In this manner, familiar melodic formulae, put together by the same principle for investigating the nature of every mode, are practiced. Of these (formulas), those for the principal modes [20] begin on their *superiores* tones (and) end on the *finales* tones. The lesser modes, however, begin and end on the *finales* tones and do not reach the range of the *superiores*, as in *Noannoeane, Noeagis,* etc., which we view less as meaningful words than as syllables associated with well-formed melody (*modulatio*).

9. WHAT THE DIFFERENCE IS BETWEEN *PHTHONGI* AND *SONI,* AND BETWEEN WHOLE TONES AND *EPOGDOI;* ALSO, WHAT TONES AND MODES OR TROPES ARE, AND ALSO *PARTICULAE;* AND WHAT INTERVAL AND SYSTEM ARE

Having learned these things above—certain preliminary exercises, as it were, and basic beginnings—we shall proceed to describe harmonic principles in an easier way. Harmony is an apt joining of different pitches. Because we do not for the most part distinguish between *soni* and *phthongi* among these pitches [21] it is necessary to explain the properties of the individual [entities] *sonus* and *phthongus, tonus* and *epogdous. Sonus* is the general name for every sound (*vox*), but we call *phthongi* the tones (*soni*) of song (*vox canora*). A *tonus* is the standard distance between two tones. This space between musical sounds, because it is in the sesquioctava proportion, is called by the Greek name *epogdous*. But when the large term exceeds the smaller by half, the proportion is called sescupla or sesquialtera or hemiola, sesquitertia when the large term is greater than the lesser by a third part, sesquiquarta when the lesser is transcended by the greater by a fourth part, sesquiquinta when the larger is greater than the other by another fifth part, sesquisexta when by a sixth part, and sesquiseptima, when by a seventh part; thus, when the high sound contains the quantity of the lower plus an additional eighth of it, the two sounds will be in the sesquioctava proportion. A semitone (*semitonium*) is not the full interval of a whole tone (*tonus*). It is sometimes called a *limma* or a *diesis*.

[22] Modes or tropes, concerning which something has been said above, are species of melodic structures, such as the authentic or plagal protus, the authentic or plagal deuterus, or the Dorian mode, the Phrygian, the Lydian, and so forth, which are terms chosen from the names of peoples. Phrases (*particulae*) of a song are its colons or commas, into which songs are divisible. Colons are properly made by joining two or more commas, although it occasionally happens that a comma and a colon cannot be distinguished

from one another. Commas are made by arsis and thesis, that is, rising and falling. Sometimes the voice is raised and lowered one time for a single arsis and thesis, but at other times more often. The space between the highest and lowest pitches of a comma is called an interval (*diastema*).[21] Such intervals may sometimes be smaller than that which we call a whole tone, at other times greater, having the interval of two, three, or sometimes several tones. Furthermore, just as the colons are composed of commas, so too [23] do we give the name *intervals* (*diastemata*) to spans within commas. Those spans that are in colons or in any whole melody we call systems (*systemata*).

10. CONCERNING THE SYMPHONIES

Not all the pitches described above blend with each other equally sweetly, nor do they produce harmonious results in song when joined together in any manner whatsoever. Just as letters, when they are randomly combined with each other, often will not make acceptable words or syllables, so too in music there are certain intervals which produce the symphonies. A symphony is a sweet combination of different pitches joined to one another. There are three simple or prime symphonies, out of which the remaining are made.[22] Of the former, they call one *diatessaron,* another *diapente,* the third *diapason.*

[24] *Diatessaron* means "through four" because it sounds either when pitches are a fourth apart or when there is an arrangement of four consecutive tones. For example, following the illustration below [figure 10.1], you may either skip down (*remittere*) to any tone a fourth away or run through four tones in a row. Thus (the tones) proceed either way[23] in four-fold variety and then recur in a new progression.

[25] *Diapente* means "through five" because it arises from a series of five consecutive tones, or because pitches a fifth apart answer concordantly to

21. 22.26–23.32 (*Discrimen . . . commatis . . . diastema . . . colis . . . sistemata*). Although this passage seems to draw its description of *diastema* from Censorinus, *De die natali* 10.3f. (Hultsch 16.26–17.2; Phillips *Sources,* pp. 273f.), what is most striking is not traceable to any earlier source: the definition of *diastema* and *systema* in terms of *comma, colon,* and *melos.* (Something similar recurs in SE, 85.371–3.) See also introduction, "Grammar and Rhetoric."

22. 23.1–7 (*Praemissae voces . . . componuntur*). Cf. Censorinus *De die natali* 10.4–6 (Hultsch 17.2–11).

23. 24.13 (*in utramvis partem*). It is not clear whether this phrase refers to the two types of progression of a given fourth (namely, by skip and by step) or to the fact that any fourth can be traversed ascending or descending (as a gloss in N suggests). If the transcription correctly reflects the intent of the *descriptio,* then *in utramvis partem* might refer to the first two intervals of each example (descending and ascending skips of a fourth, respectively), which precede the "new" scalar progression of the same species of fourth. In that case, "in either way" could be replaced with a less ambiguous "in both directions."

Figure 10.1

each other,[24] as illustrated in figure 10.2. A symphony can be designated a diapente when, as in this diagram, you lead the individual tones in order—both rising and falling, or in only one direction—from any of the four tones to one a fifth away, which has the same name. Furthermore, if you sing the [two] groups of four examples of figure 10.3, there will be a consonant correspondence at the fifth,[25] which is more particularly characteristic of the diapente. [26]

Likewise the *diapason,* which means "through all," is made by the agree-

24. 25.16 (*a quinto loco concordes sibi voces respondeant*). The verb *respondere* is used in the *Enchiriadis* treatises in two senses: (1) in a monophonic context to indicate a relationship between two successive notes, the second "answering" the first; and (2) in a polyphonic context to indicate vertical and temporal "correspondence" between two simultaneously sounding notes. These two meanings have a parallel in rhetorical discourse. Cf. Heinrich Lausberg, *Handbuch der literarischen Rhetorik* (Munich: Max Hueber, 1970), 2:799, where *respondere* is said to mean, depending on context, *antworten* or *entsprechen.*

25. 25.22 (*idem consonanter quinta regione respondet*). This phrase does not necessarily imply simultaneous performance of the upper and lower melodies of figs. 10.3 and 10.4, although *respondere* later is often used (beginning at 38.13) in connection with organum. The point of figs. 10.3 and 10.4 is that the distance between corresponding tones of the higher and lower groups of melodic phrases remains constant. A "symphony" is a symphony whether its constituent elements sound successively or simultaneously.

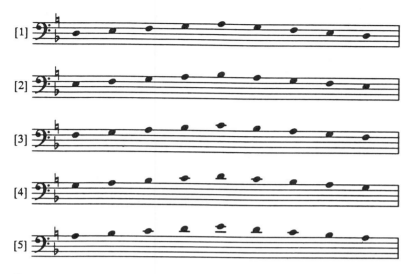

Figure 10.2

Figure 10.3

ment (*consonantia*) of tones an octave apart, containing in its system the two symphonies discussed above. This symphony is said to be "through all" because the ancients did not use more than eight strings.[26] In this symphony the pitches can be said to be not so much "sounding well together" (*consonae*) as "equal-sounding" (*aequisonae*), for in this symphony a pitch is revealed anew. This may be seen most readily with musical instruments, but, if they are not at hand, [27] one [singer] may sustain a pitch on any tone

26. 26.26–7 (*quod antiqui non plus quam octo cordis utebantur*). The literary tradition that the Greek kithara had only eight strings is also asserted in SE (90.8f.). However, a reexamination of the literary and archeological evidence by Martha Maas and Jane McIntosh Snyder, *Stringed Instruments of Ancient Greece* (New Haven and London: Yale University Press, 1989), p. 203, concludes that the kithara, properly speaking, never had more than seven strings.

while another goes through two groups of four [pitches] in order, either ascending or descending. When the last has sounded, you will perceive that it produces complete consonance with the first, an octave away. Therefore, when one sings (*modulari*) using such equal-sounding pitches, it is done in a combination of this kind [figure 10.4].[27]

Figure 10.4

11. HOW OUT OF SIMPLE SYMPHONIES OTHERS ARE COMPOUNDED

[28] Out of these simple symphonies others are put together, such as the diapason-plus-diatesseron, diapason-plus-diapente, and disdiapason, also called the disdiplasion. For example, if to two men's voices sounding together at the diapason there is added a third voice—that of a boy at equal-sounding [pitch]—the highest and lowest among them produce a disdiapason, which symphony the two corresponding pitches sound together at the fifteenth. The middle voice, however, answers the two others at the diapason as figure 11.1 shows. [29]

[31] To be sure, a consonance is not made from just any tone to the fourth or fifth or to the octave. However, nearly all individual tones answer with the diatessaron at the fourth tone both above and below, and all answer with the diapente at the fifth tone. And every tone sounds the diapason at

27. 27.*descriptio* 4 (fig. 10.4). The letters in the left-hand column of the original diagram are not letter names of specific tones; rather, they are employed to indicate octave equivalence: the two tones labeled "A" are an octave apart. Only the upper voice has daseian symbols; the lower voice has none since, to maintain perfect octaves throughout, it must sound pitches not in the daseian scale, a situation that did not arise in figure 10.3. A similar use of letters is found in 32.*descriptio* 2 (fig. 11.2). But a corresponding example in SE at 91.*descriptio* 1 (fig. 27) is somewhat different: the opening pitches are labeled with the first, eighth, and fifteenth letters of the Latin alphabet A, H, and P (I and J are not counted as separate letters) to indicate the octave and double-octave intervals separating the tones. Moreover, the letters of the two examples in ME descend, whereas those in the SE example ascend.

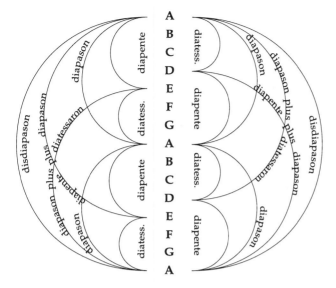

Figure 11.1

the eighth tone away on either side.[28] These last—the eighth tones on both sides, thus a diapason to the middle tone—sound in turn a disdiapason at the fifteenth, as has been said.

It happens that the span of a diapason is always filled by a diatessaron and a diapente. For while on either side the two middle tones in this span answer with the diatessaron and diapente, it turns out that when one of them makes the diapente on one side, it makes a diatessaron on the other, and that which makes a diatessaron on one side will make a diapente on the other. Thus the largest symphony is made up of two smaller ones. Furthermore, the largest symphony is called "diapason" because its consonance is more perfect than that of the others, such that, whether you begin high or low, the pitch to which you will change at the octave above or below will have oneness of sound with the first pitch when sung as in figure 11.2.[29] [32]

28. 31.11–2 (*sonus quisque in utramque partem ad octavum a se sonum diapason resonat*). This is not strictly true for every tone within the *Enchiriadis* scale, of course. Accordingly, N glosses *diapason* with *scil. pene* ("that is, *almost* [every tone sounds the diapason at the eighth tone away]"). The author of ME, however, is preparing the way for a quotation from Boethius, in whose system the octaves are consistent.

29. 32.*descriptio* 2 (fig. 11.2). The melody and text here constitute the fifteenth verse of the *Te Deum*. The pitch level and mode are not inferrable from ME's text and illustration, since the letters do not represent pitch, although it is clear that the principal voice is the middle one and

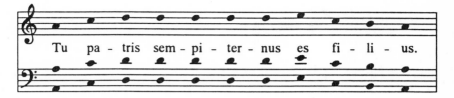

Figure 11.2

Thus the natural sequence of tones proceeds unendingly, as if reborn at the octave from each tone, so that I say that a new series emerges [33] in the voice and, as in the law of days, the eighth is that which is the first, the first is that which is the eighth. Thus, in Vergil, Orpheus at Elysium "accompanies with seven different pitches," [30] because, of course, the series of sounds is continued using seven different pitches and, an octave away, shifts into a new (series).

> For just as when an integer contained within the number 10 is preserved whole and inviolate when added to it—although this never happens with other numbers—so also is it in this context. For if you add 2 to 3 you produce 5 immediately, and the species [31] of number is changed. But if you add them to 10 you will make 12, and the 2 is preserved, joined to the 10—likewise 3 and others in the same way. Therefore, just as the symphony of the diapason preserves another consonance which it contains, it neither changes it nor produces a dissonance out of something consonant. [32]

Thus it happens that just as [two] tones blend consonantly at the fifteenth, which is two octaves, so too any tone sounds a diapente from the octave to the twelfth, as if [from itself] to a fifth. Similarly a diatessaron sounds at the eleventh as if at the fourth. In this an extraordinary relationship must also be noted, namely, that if tones a ninth apart are compared—whether

---

that the others are understood to follow at perfect octaves throughout. Thus the transcriptions here and at 39.*descriptio* (fig. 14.1) have been made in a D mode transposed up a fifth for convenience of singing. However, this same melody is given at five specific pitch levels (i.e., four different modes) in the succeeding *descriptiones* that use it on 35f., 38, and 53–5 (figs. 12.1–2, 13.1, and 18.2–5).

30. 33.27–8. The oft cited phrase *septem discrimina vocum* is from *Aen.* 6.646.

31. 33.33 (*species*). Phillips *Sources*, p. 244, suggests that *species* should be interpreted as "visual appearance."

32. 33.29–36. This passage is taken virtually verbatim from Boethius *De inst. mus.* 5.10 (Friedlein 360.7–17); the sentence following in the translation (33.37–9) paraphrases material from the remainder of Boethius *De inst. mus.* 5.10 based on Ptolemy, *Harmonics* 1.6. Although the numbers are actually expressed in words by both Boethius and ME, arabic numerals have been used in the translation to make the point visually clearer. Roman numerals would serve equally well.

by singing one directly after the other (*absolute*) or by stepping through the ordered series of tones separating them—[34] they will be found to be the same; but [this is not true of] those eight steps apart.[33] And yet, not only in the symphony of the diapason, which spans an octave, but also in the dis-diapason, the octaves are made equivalent by a wondrous change (*mutatio mirabilis*).

12. MORE CONCERNING THESE SYMPHONIES

The four individual tones (*quattuor moduli*) in which the first symphony, called the diatessaron, is found, differ from one another by the agreeable diversity of their properties, and this harmonious assemblage is constructed, as has been said, using the tetrachord as the basis. And so, with four at a time following one another continuously, it is inevitable that tones a fifth apart are always of the same type;[34] and it is also evident that, as has been shown, when tones a fifth apart, [and thus] of the same type or quality, are put together, they answer each other in a symphony which is called the diapente. Something concerning its nature, and also other things, has already been made known. Nevertheless, so that what is dealt with next can be explained more clearly, [35] the principle of the diapente is conveyed by reflecting on figure 12.1, which again uses lines. As before, let there be a series of straight lines from the signs for the tones that have been written down, and let the symphony of the diapente be represented on the lines.

Tu pa - tris sem - pi - ter - nus es   fi - li - us.

Figure 12.1

When, according to the principle of this illustration, one [sign] after another is accurately sung a fifth apart, you will perceive that they accord

33. 34.42 (*idem inveniuntur noni ad nonos, non octavi ad octavam*). That tones a ninth apart have the same name and properties, whereas those eight steps apart do not, is supported by eleventh-century glosses in *P* and *Ca* that refer to the sameness of the daseian symbols a ninth apart. Another possible interpretation, which would assume that the consistency of interval is the principal issue here, is that all ninths are the same, i.e., an octave plus a whole tone, whereas some octaves are perfect and others augmented.

34. 34.5 (*eiusdem conditionis*). Previously (at 4.10, 4.22, and 6.1) this phrase has referred to "similarly constituted" tetrachords. Here, however, the author is speaking of tones of similar attributes a fifth apart. The author of a gloss in *N* finds this similarity to reside "in the name and note-form."

respectively with one another in the same type of quality at the symphony of the diapente. Because a natural principle imparts an individual quality to each of the four elemental tones through the four-fold disposition of the tones and semitones, it cannot happen that some melody can maintain the same constitution or mode if it is transposed from one set of tones to another. We have touched on this somewhat in the sections above and now must elaborate it more fully by means of additional examples.

[36] A series of lines is extended [in figure 12.2] just as above, and the same melody, which is now represented within the symphony of the fifth, is rendered in four or five examples in (different) colors.[35] You will see that the form of a melody cannot be exactly preserved in transposition but is changed from one mode to another when shifted by a whole tone or semitone.

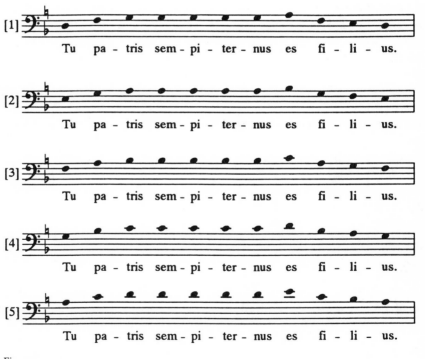

Figure 12.2

35. 36.21–3 (*idem melos . . . quarternis vel quinis colorum descriptionibus exprimatur*). Schmid's note to 36.9f. indicates that ten manuscripts utilize colors for *descriptiones* 1–4 (figs. 12.1–4). See also note to 14.10 above. For a diplomatic transcription of an illustration in similar format, see figur 8.2.

Take the first illustration, which begins and ends on the tone *Ϝ* and is considered to be in the first mode. If you put the whole melody one space higher, so that it is drawn on the blank area (*paginula*) between the two lines, then it is changed into the deuterus mode, which begins on the tone *Ϝ* and ends on the same. [37] Do this two spaces higher, beginning on the tone *Γ*, and it will be the tritus mode. At three spaces, the fourth mode will be born. If this is done one space higher, the first mode will emerge anew at the fifth. Similarly in the others: a prior arrangement always recurs at the fifth.

13. CONCERNING THE PROPERTIES OF THE SYMPHONIES

It has now been shown how every tone in a tetrachord is different from the others by virtue of its relative position (*propria conditio*) and how from the agreeable diversity of these tones the different species of modes or tropes are produced. At what distances from one another pitches consequently produce the individual symphonies has also been related. Now, however, we proceed with what the symphonies are and are properly called, that is, how these same pitches conduct themselves when sung simultaneously. Indeed, this is what we call diaphony, that is, two-voiced song or, customarily, *organum*. Diaphony is so called because it does not consist in unison singing[36] but in an agreeable combination of different pitches. Although commonly used for all the symphonies, this name applies [properly] to [simultaneous singing at] the diatessaron and diapente.

[38] To begin, an example of organal music[37] at the diatessaron is given [figure 13.1]. According to this illustration, one voice corresponds to another singing simultaneously a fourth away, two tones being between them.[38]

Tu pa - tris sem - pi - ter - nus es fi - li - us.

Figure 13.1

36. 37.8 (*uniformi canore*). "Unison" here should probably be understood as encompassing not only monophonic performance by more than one voice in unison but also singing in octaves (which produces a sound designated *unisona* at 31.22).

37. 38.11 (*organici meli*). Regarding this phrase, see introduction, "The Putative Relationship to Johannes Scottus Eriugena."

38. 38.13 (*vox voci*). The term *vox* now takes on an important new meaning: it now begins to signify an entire succession of tones, a "voice" as in part-writing. Perhaps this new meaning was suggested by the uses of *vox* in grammatical theory for both a single sound and a complete sentence or utterance.

Thus, in the simultaneous singing of two or more voices with the restrained and agreeable slowness that is characteristic of this music, you will perceive smooth concord born of this mixture of tones.

14. CONCERNING DIAPHONY DOUBLED (*AUCTIOR*) AT THE DIATESSARON, AND AN ILLUSTRATION OF IT

Not only may a single voice be joined to a single voice in this combination [at the fourth]; also, a single organum (*simplex organum*) may have correspondence with a doubled [principal] voice, and a doubled [organal voice] may have correspondence with a single [principal voice].[39] [39] If you duplicate both [voices] at the octave, you will hear that pitches in these relationships sound sweetly with each other, as shown in figure 14.1.[40]

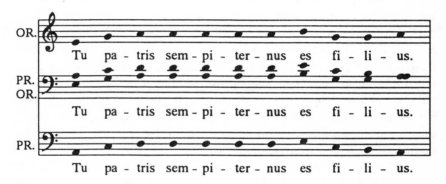

Figure 14.1

[Here is an] explanation of this illustration: Mutual concord will be produced by the principle illustrated, if [i] you join a doubled organum (*duplex organum*) to an undoubled melody (*simplex cantus*), [40] the former being represented by the first [topmost] and third lines, which stand in the relationship of organum to the second line; or [ii] an undoubled organum (*simplex organum*) is brought into a relationship with a doubled melody, the latter being designated by the second and fourth lines, which contain the organum between them; or [iii] you double both organum and melody, or [iv] you triple them. For human voices can be mixed with one another and with some musical instruments, not only two and two but also three and three in this combination, provided that, whether with one sound or with three

39. 38.2 (*organum*). Here, and often in the subsequent chapters, *organum* means "the organal voice," not the practice of simultaneous singing called "organum".

40. 39.*descriptio* (fig. 14.1). See note to 32.*descriptio* 2 (fig. 11.2).

pitches employed simultaneously, the same number of pitches correspond as organum.

Here it must be noted that the middle voice between two [organal voices] is not equally distant from them. This is because the [middle voice] has correspondence at a diatessaron below but at a diapente above, just as there is no integral midpoint in the number 8. This may be introduced more clearly to novices without wearying the learned: If a man and a boy sing simultaneously as organal voices, [41] the two make a diapason with each other. However, the higher [voice], which is the boy's, is heard a fifth above, and the lower [voice], which is the man's, is heard a fourth below that middle voice which they contain between each other and to which both correspond as organum. Thus the symphonies bind themselves together by means of a mutual relationship, so that any tone that lies a fourth from another on one side looks at the other an octave away from the distance of a fifth.

15. AN ILLUSTRATION OF DIAPHONY DOUBLED
AT THE DIAPENTE

In turn, whenever diaphony at the fifth is accurately sung by three or four voices, a voice that is a fifth below the middle voice will, when doubled at the diapason, necessarily have correspondence at the fourth above the middle voice, as in figure 15.1.[41]

[42] [Here is an] explanation of this illustration. The four-fold series of this illustration is disposed in the same arrangement as above [figure 14.1]. The first [topmost] and third lines [43] correspond as organum to the middle line. The second and fourth lines, themselves at the consonance diapason, combine with the undoubled organum, the third voice, which is in the middle. Additionally, [the illustration] shows doubled organum (*geminum organum*) with doubled melody. Also, you see where the third line is joined to the second line at the fifth below, and the third and fourth lines and the

---

41. Schmid 42.*descriptio* (fig. 15.1). The transcription given here adopts the proposal in Phillips *Sources*, p. 459, that the daseian symbols to the left of the uppermost voice actually belong to the next voice below. (Her transcription is, however, given as sounding one octave higher.) Were the transcription to follow precisely the illustration in Schmid's edition (and the latter is faithful to his editorial principles), then the upper and lower pairs of voices would open with a tritone, or else the principal voices would sing F♯s that are not in the *Enchiriadis* pitch set. The present transcription avoids such problems by assuming that the uppermost voice doubles the main organal voice an octave above and that the lowest voice doubles the main principal voice an octave below. Such doubling voices are expected to maintain the octave throughout—by invoking the "wondrous change" cited at the end of chap. 11 (34.44)—and are not restricted to the notes of the *Enchiriadis* pitch set.

Figure 15.1

first and second, respectively, sound together (*consonare*) at a distance of a fourth. For these reasons, these two symphonies blend together different, sweet melodies.

16. WHAT BOETHIUS SAYS PTOLEMY THOUGHT ABOUT THESE THINGS

Here we can observe that the assertion of Ptolemy is seen to be true, for Boethius tells how he [Ptolemy] disagreed with the Pythagoreans, who say the diapason-plus-diatessaron is not a consonance. But surely when you sing either of these illustrations [figures 14.1 and 15.1], doubling both melody and organum, doubled voice is combined with doubled voice, just as a single voice may be added to a single voice. Also, if singing simultaneously the second and fourth [voice] of the first illustration [figure 14.1] you also join a fifth [voice] at the fourth below, [44] a diatessaron sounds with the diapason, duly and simply. Let us sing, according to the prior illustration [figure 15.1], the fourth and second [voices], adding also the first; the same conso-

nance [the diatessaron] likewise sounds with the diapason. The great teacher
mentioned above [Boethius], in the fifth book of his explanation of music,
proceeds from the opinion of Ptolemy in this way, placing high sounds in
the farther [lower] end, the low ones on the nearer [higher], as in figure 16.1.

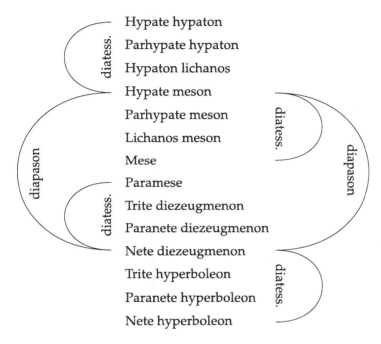

Hypate hypaton
Parhypate hypaton
Hypaton lichanos
Hypate meson
Parhypate meson
Lichanos meson
Mese
Paramese
Trite diezeugmenon
Paranete diezeugmenon
Nete diezeugmenon
Trite hyperboleon
Paranete hyperboleon
Nete hyperboleon

Figure 16.1

[45] He [Boethius] says[42]

the consonance of the diapason makes such a conjunction of pitch that it seems
to come from one and the same string—as the Pythagoreans also agree; for this
reason, if a consonance is added to [the diapason], [the consonance] is preserved
whole and inviolate. So also the diatessaron is added to the consonance of the
diapason as if to one string. Let there be a consonance diapason, which extends

42. 45.14–47.39. This extended passage from Boethius *De inst. mus.* 5.9 (Friedlein 358.22–
360.4) gives the Ptolemaic reasoning for why the eleventh (represented mathematically by the
ratio 8:3) is a consonance, a position that contradicts the Pythagorean belief that only multiple and superparticular ratios may underlie consonances. (Cf. Ptolemy *Harmonics* 1.6, trans.
Andrew Barker, *Greek Musical Writings* (Cambridge: Cambridge University Press, 1984–
1989), 2:286–88.) The Ptolemaic rationalization is necessary to justify octave doublings in
organum at the fourth. Octave doublings in organum at the fifth create no problem, since the
ratio corresponding to the twelfth is 3:1, a multiple.

between hypate meson [E] and nete diezeugmenon [e]. The tones thus accord with each other and are so united that one pitch (*vox*)—as if produced by one string, not of two mixed together—strikes the hearing. Therefore, whatever consonance we join to this diapason consonance is preserved whole because it is joined as if to one tone (*vocula*) and string. If, therefore, to hypate meson [E] and nete diezeugmenon [e] [46] are joined the diatessarons above each—namely, if that which is nete hyperboleon [a'] is joined to nete diezeugmenon [e], and that which is mese [a] is joined to hypate meson [E]—then each will agree with the other, as also mese [a] with nete diezeugmenon [e] and the same mese [a] with hypate meson [E]—likewise nete hyperboleon [a'] with nete diezeugmenon [e], and also with hypate meson [E]. If to the lower side of each is added a consonance of the diatessaron, there will indeed be to the hypate meson [E] a consonance of the diatessaron, namely hypate hypaton [B], and on the other hand [there will be] to nete diezeugmenon [e] [a consonance] paramese [b]. Hypate hypaton [B] and hypate meson [E] will join with nete diezeugmenon [e], [47] whereas nete diezeugmenon [e] and hypate meson [E] will sound together with paramese [b],[43] but in a manner such that the tone which is lower retains the consonance diatessaron as the closest consonance and [the consonance] diatessaron-plus-diapason to the farther tone, as the diatessaron [formed by] hypate hypaton [B] to hypate meson [E] and the diatessaron-plus-diapason [formed] to nete diezeugmenon [e]. Likewise, nete hyperboleon [a'], which is higher, sounds together with nete diezeugmenon [e], the nearest diatessaron to it, but [forms] the diatessaron-plus-diapason to hypate meson [E], and so on.

Thus says Boethius.

17. [CONCERNING THE ORDER OF THE CONSONANCES AND WHAT CONSTITUTES CONSONANCE AND INCONSONANCE]

Beyond this there is no need to illustrate the diapason and the disdiapason, which occur so naturally in singing at every age that they do not have to be taught through art. It has been sufficiently explained that in the symphony of the disdiapason [48] the middle occurs an octave away from both [extremes], and that the extremes have correspondence with each other at the fifteenth. The proper size of the individual symphonies needs to be mentioned, however. The symphony of the diatessaron consists of two whole

---

43. 46.32–47.33. The wording of ME differs slightly from that of Friedlein's edition of Boethius *De inst. mus.* 5.9 (Friedlein 359.18–20). ME: *Consonabitque et hypate hypaton et hypate meson ad neten diezeugmenon, ad paramesen autem nete diezeugmenon et hypate meson.* Friedlein: *consonabitque et hypate hypaton, ad hypaten meson et ad neten diezeugmenon et paramese ad neten diezeugmenon et ad hypaten meson.*

tones and a semitone, [that of] the diapente of three whole tones and a semitone, and these two comprise the symphony of the diapason. Therefore,
different pitches sound most completely together with greater perfection in
the symphony of the diapason than in the others. Second in perfection is
the symphony of the diapente. But in the diatessaron, tones do not agree
sweetly with each other at the fourth throughout the entire series of tones,
and consequently symphonic song (*simphoniaca cantilena*) does not result
so consistently as in the others. Thus, in this kind of song, by a certain law
of its own,[44] pitches are wondrously adjusted to others. For in the entire
series of tones only the tritus, the fourth below the deuterus, is not symphonic and is rendered inconsonant with it [the deuterus], because the tritus
alone is located three whole tones from the deuterus (*praefatus sonus*). This
exceeds the size of the symphony of the diatessaron, which is at the fourth
below. [49] For this reason, a voice which is called "organal" customarily
accompanies another voice called "principal" such that, in any tetrachord in
any musical phrase (*particula*), [the organal voice] neither descends below
the tetrardus tone at the end (*positio*) nor rises at the beginning (*inchoatio*).
This is because of the obstructing inconsonance of the tritus tone, which is
the second below the tetrardus tone. To make these things clearer, they are
illustrated in an example, insofar as it can be made visible [figure 17.1].[45]

Rex   cae - li   do - mi - ne   ma - ris   un - di - so - ni.

Ty - tan - is   ni - ti - di   qual - li - di - que   so - li.

Figure 17.1

When singing according to this illustration it is easily perceived how, [50]
in the two phrases (*membra*) illustrated, an organal pitch cannot begin its
correspondence under the tetrardus tone, nor can it legally descend below
this same tone at the end. On account of this an organal voice is absorbed
by the principal pitch as both come together as one at the very end.

44. 48.13 (*sua quadam lege*). For other references in ME and SE to the special "law" gov-
erning organum, see 52.18, 52.26, and 97.54f.

45. 49.*descriptio* (fig. 17.1). See note to 12.*descriptio* (fig. 7.1).

18. HOW ORGANUM PROCEEDS AT HIGHER AND LOWER LEVELS

Because of the impediment of the limit mentioned above, the organal voice is compressed into a short space and has a range of only three or four tones. For that reason it changes according to the ending (*positio*) and range (*loca*) of the phrases. For as the phrases roam about, the melody sometimes proceeds upwards and sometimes falls downwards; a phrase on one occasion may end in the superiores [tones], on another in the finales, and sometimes among the graves. Nonetheless, at phrase [beginnings and] endings an organal voice conforms to this law: namely, the organal voice is not properly permitted to begin an ascent, or to descend to the end, below a tetrardus tone on which the phrase ends or which is the tetrardus just below the last note of the principal voice. [51] By way of example, a chant previously selected [is elaborated in figure 18.1].

Te hu‑mi‑les fa‑mu‑li mo‑du‑lis ve‑ne‑ran‑do pi‑is.

Se iu‑be‑as fla‑gi‑tant va‑ri‑is li‑be‑ra‑re ma‑lis.

Figure 18.1

In the two phrases just treated [figure 17.1], *Rex caeli domine maris un-disoni* and *Tytanis nitidi squalidique soli,* the first three syllables [*Rex caeli* and *Tytanis*] [52] that sound tetrardus ⅂ [C], archous Ϝ [D], and deuterus Ϝ [E] do not have an organal correspondence under tetrardus, specifically on account of the inconsonance of the deuterus tone [E] to the tritus tone [Bb] that is immediately below the tetrardus. So too in the following commas [figure 18.1] *Te humiles famuli* and *Se iubeas flagitant:*[46] whereas the rise and fall of the commas are seen at a higher level than at figure 17.1, the organum is also confined to a higher locus by the same law. Similarly, in the three principal tones, the tetrardus Ϝ [G], archous ꓩ[a], and deuterusꓩ [b], the organal voice is unable to have correspondence in a proper manner under the tetrardus tone, but dwells on it, since at the second below [F] it does have a valid correspondence [at the fourth above].

So that it may be understood clearly how much the inconsonance of the

46. 52.17 (*commatibus*). *Comma* is defined in chap. 9 (22.21ff.).

two tones named above [tritus and deuterus] rules the symphony of the diatessaron, let us decide to sing something in four different transpositions. Then it will be apparent how in the different transpositions one voice may accompany another in a different manner, but not according to a different law.

[53] Take the first illustration [figure 13.1]—one that has also been considered above—wherein the organal voice proceeds simultaneously with the principal voice, which begins and ends on the tone $ƒ$ [D].

Tu   pa - tris   sem - pi - ter - nus   es   fi - li - us.

Figure 18.2

When singing in this way [figure 18.2], you perceive how the ascent of the organal voice, not obstructed by the dissonance of the deuterus $ƒ$ [E] and tritus $⋀$ [B♭], is placed consonantly at the fourth below. However, the descent [of the organal voice] does not go below the tetrardus [C] because of the impediment of that same dissonance.

[54] Let us now take up the second transposition [figure 18.3], which be-

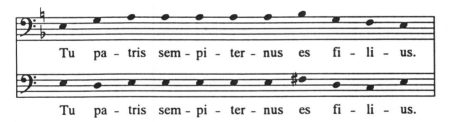

Tu   pa - tris   sem - pi - ter - nus   es   fi - li - us.

Tu   pa - tris   sem - pi - ter - nus   es   fi - li - us.

Figure 18.3

gins and ends on the same tone, $ƒ$ [E].[47] Singing in this way, you perceive how an organal correspondence is lacking on the deuterus tone $ƒ$ [E] both at

47. 54.*descriptio* 3 (fig. 18.3). Although there is a tritone on the word *es*, undoubtedly the F in the organal voice would be raised in performance to preserve the perfect fourth between the voices. Waeltner, *Die Lehre vom Organum*, pp. 14f., puts the organal voice on that syllable a step higher (on A) but can cite only one eleventh-century manuscript as support. Phillips *Sources*, pp. 321f., raises the possibility that fig. 18.3 is a musical representation of the procession from and return to the One taught by John Scotus. The relationship of ME to ninth-century Neoplatonism is discussed in the introduction.

the ascent and at the descent[48] and, for this reason, does not descend beyond the tetrardus 𝄖 [C].

Let us now take up the third transposition [figure 18.4], which begins

Tu pa - tris sem - pi - ter - nus es   fi - li - us.

Figure 18.4

and ends on the tritus tone ⌐ [F]. [55] Since this transposition proceeds with emphasis on the deuterus tone ⌐ [b], it does not admit of an appropriate organal correspondence.

Let us take up the fourth transposition [figure 18.5], which begins on

Tu pa - tris sem - pi - ter - nus es   fi - li - us.

Figure 18.5

tetrardus 𝄎 [G] and ends on the same. You thus perceive how, in singing, the organal voice begins and ends on the tetrardus tone 𝄎 [G] but is unable to progress below this to the tritus ⌐ [F], specifically because of that obstructing tone which, as now has often been said, is dissonant with the deuterus [b].

[56] There has been outlined here some basic information about musical art for the adornment of ecclesiastical songs;[49] certainly, this [science] also bears no less respectful study in a deeper way. For why some tones agree with each other in a sweet commingling, whereas others disagree unpleasantly, being unwilling to blend with each other, has a rather profound and divine explanation, and in some respects is among the most hidden things of nature. This principle, whose operations in this realm (*in hac parte*) the Lord also permits us to penetrate, is treated in the writings of the ancients. In these is asserted, with most convincing arguments, that the same guiding principle that controls the concord of pitches regulates the natures of mor-

48. 54.37. Waeltner, *Die Lehre vom Organum*, p. 15, argues (not unreasonably) that *et in levatione et in positione* refers to the beginning and end of the phrase, rather than the rise and fall of the principal voice.

49. 56.49 (*Superficies quaedam artis musicae*). Possibly the model for the use of the term *superficies* was Boethius *De inst. mus.* 1.33 (Friedlein 223.2).

tals. Through these numerical relationships, by which unlike sounds concord with each other, the eternal harmony of life and of the conflicting elements of the whole world is united as one with material things.

19. WHY THE PROFUNDITY OF THIS PRINCIPLE MAY BE LESS PENETRABLE IN SOME THINGS[50]

[57] The ancients tell that Aristeus was in love with the nymph Eurydice, spouse of Orpheus. While fleeing her pursuer (Aristeus), she was killed by a snake. We perceive an Orpheus whose name signifies *oreo phone*—"the best voice"—in a skilled singer (*cantor peritus*) or in sweet-sounding melody. If any "good man,"[51] as *Aristeus* may be translated, pursues [Orpheus's] Eurydice—that is, "profound understanding"—out of love, he is hindered by divine wisdom, lest she be entirely possessed, as if by the snake. But while she in turn is called forth from her hidden places and from the underworld by Orpheus, that is, by the most noble sound of song, she is seemingly led up into the atmosphere of this life and, as soon as she seems to be seen, is lost.

So, as in other things that we discern only partly and dimly, this discipline does not at all have a full, comprehensible explanation in this life. To be sure, we can judge whether the construction of a melody is proper and distinguish the qualities of tones and modes and the other things of this art. Likewise, we can adduce, on the basis of numbers, the musical intervals or [58] the symphonies of pitches and give some explanations of consonance and dissonance. But in what way music has so great an affinity and union (*commutatio et societas*) with our souls—for we know that we are bound to it by a certain likeness[52]—we cannot express easily in words.

50. 57.1ff. Whether chap. 19 really belongs to ME is discussed in the introduction, "Organization."

51. 57.5–6 (*vir bonus quod Aristeus interpretatur*). The phrase *vir bonus* would have immediately suggested to the medieval reader schooled in rhetorical theory all the qualities associated with the ideal orator; in Quintilian, for example, the phrase recurs again and again, beginning with the preface to book 1, section 9 (Butler translation, p. 9), and carries implications of exemplary moral behavior, skillful delivery, and breadth of education—qualities that SE in particular seems to seek in a *peritus cantor*. The characterizations of Orpheus and Eurydice respectively (57.3–5) as "best voice" (*oreo phone*) and "profound understanding" (*profunda diiudicatio*) are from Fulgentius, *Mitologiae* 3.10, the principal source for the allegory in chap. 19 (see Fabius Planciades Fulgentius, *Opera*, ed. Rudolf Helm [Stuttgart: Teubner, 1970], 77). The association of Aristeus with *vir bonus*, however, seems to be unique to chap. 19 of ME. For arguments regarding the authorship and dating of ME on the basis of the various Carolingian versions of this myth, see Phillips *Sources*, pp. 384–90, and Peter Dronke, "The Beginnings of the Sequence," *Beiträge der deutschen Sprache und Literatur* 87 (Tübingen, 1965):43–73, especially 70–3.

52. 58.16–8. Cf. Boethius, *De inst. mus.* 1.1 (Friedlein 180.8f.).

We can judge melody not only by the inherent naturalness of the tones but also [by that] of the subjects (*res*). For it is necessary that the affections (*affectus*) of the subjects that are sung [about] correspond to the expression (*effectus*) of the song, so that melodies (*neumae*) are peaceful in tranquil subjects, joyful in happy matters, somber in sad [ones], [and] harsh things are said or made to be expressed by harsh melodies. Similarly, let melodies be misshapen, sudden, noisy, excited, and designed for other qualities of affections and events. Furthermore, let phrases of melodies and of words end simultaneously.[53] Although our judgment can be exercised in such matters, there are many [things] the explanations of which are hidden in secrecy from us. Sometimes there are subjects that can be admitted for singing equally in one mode (*tonus*) or another. But sometimes there are subjects that simply do not express their content (*sensus*) through just any mode, so that [melodies], [59] if put in another mode, either do not preserve their earlier sweetness or else they offend the senses. Wild animals and birds are said to be attracted by certain modes more than others, but it is not easily investigated how and why such things are.

Therefore, those aspects of this art which, thanks to God, we understand, let us use in the praise of the Lord; and in rejoicing, celebrating, [and] singing, let us adopt those things which have been discovered for us by the laborious investigations of the ancients—things which in prior generations were not known to the sons of men but now have been revealed to his saints. That most eminent author Boethius relates many marvelous things about the principles of music, proving all of them simply by the authority of numbers. Of this, if God grant it, the little work following [the *Scolica enchiriadis*] will contain some portion. Let us, then, put an end here to this little discourse.

---

53. 58.25 (*in unum*). If organum is not implied by this phrase, it is the only instance where *in unum* is used in ME or SE without reference to polyphonic performance.

Scolica enchiriadis

[P A R T 1]

[P A R T 1]

M[aster]. What is music?[1]

D[isciple]. The science of regulating properly the movement of sound.[2]

M. But what does it mean to regulate properly the movement of sound?

D. To control melody so that it sounds sweet. But this must be done in full conformance with the rules (*ad artem*). It is clear to me that one who misuses the sweetness of this art for worthless purposes, just as one who does not know how to apply [the rules of] the discipline (*ars*) where it is necessary, does not regulate sound properly. Rather, only someone with a heart full of devotion sings sweetly to the Lord.

M. You are right in thinking that sweet melodies are well-made only when they serve

---

1. 60, title *Scolica enchiriadis*. See introduction, *"Scolica enchiriadis."*

2. 60.1 (M: *Musica quid est?* D: *Bene modulandi scientia..*) This definition of *musica* originated (at least in its Latin formulation) in the lost *Disciplinae* of Marcus Terentius Varro (116–27 B.C.), the first known Latin writer on music. It reappeared in *De die natali* 10.3 of Censorinus, *De Musica* 1.2.2 of Augustine, and *Institutiones* 2.5.2 of Cassiodorus, as well as in modified form in the *Etymologiae* 3.15 of Isidore of Seville and the *Musica Disciplina* 2.1 of Aurelian, before being employed so very prominently as the opening of SE. The most extensive explanation of the definition occurs in the first book of Augustine's *De Musica*, which was undoubtedly the model for SE. There "music" (i.e., the *ars musica*, the liberal art of music) is defined as *scientia bene modulandi*. *Modulari* does not mean *simply* "to sing" but implies regulating sound with an accuracy and awareness informed by the mathematical laws underlying the discipline of music. For a detailed historical survey of *modulari, modulatio,* and other related terms, see Christoph von Blumröder, "Modulatio/Modulation," *HdMT* (1983).

a good purpose and, likewise, that sacred melodies are not used properly if they are performed unpleasantly without theoretical knowledge (*disciplina*). Therefore, since this knowledge is indeed most necessary for ecclesiastical songs, lest they be disfigured by carelessness or ignorance, let us see what things are necessary for the ability to regulate sound properly.

D. I see that there are many things that a cantor [61] must observe; if he has no knowledge of them, he cannot be expert. But it is reserved to you to expound these things with greater specificity.

M. There are some things demanded by the properties of tones, other things which are required by the principle of rhythm, and still other things outside [the discipline] [3] to which the science of singing aptly conforms.

D. What are these "tones" (*soni*)?

M. Here we call tones *phthongi*, that is, the agreeable-sounding tones (*voculae*) of song, which constitute the foundation of harmony. For just as a word consists of letters, so does harmony consist of phthongi.

D. What are those things which the properties of tones demand?

M. That no discord (*absonia*) be made in them by violating their natural quality.

D. What causes this discord among phthongi?

M. Singing them either lower or higher than is proper. Both the quality of the tones and the whole chant are debased by this first fault in human voices. This happens when what is sung either is lowered by a spiritless sinking [of pitch] or is improperly forced too high. This error cannot happen in musical instruments because the pitch of the individual tones remains fixed once the disposition of the tones has been established.

Another type of discord (*dissonantia*) occurs when the distance between two tones is falsely measured, that is, when one tone is put for another. The third type of discord occurs when a tone does not answer another [62] at the interval it should. These last two errors have the same cause, but they differ in this: the former is made within a single melody, the latter in initiating and answering.[4]

---

3. 61.14 (*extrinsecus occurrentibus*). This puzzling phrase (and its counterpart at 89.424f.) has been interpreted variously. Gustav Jacobsthal, *Die chromatische Alteration im liturgischen Gesang der abendländischen Kirche* (Berlin, 1897), p. 247f., proposes that it may refer to vocal ornaments like the quilisma. Phillips *Sources*, p. 146, suggests that the reference is to organum, which is treated extensively in SE, part 2 (but see the note to 89.424f.). Further expanding the possibilities are glosses in two eleventh-century manuscripts. N has *ut bona vox* ("such as a good voice") and P has *eae sunt laetisonae causae vel tristes, quod in laetisonis causis laetae neumae, in tristibus tristes debent fore* ("There are joyful- or sad-sounding contexts, since in joyful-sounding contexts the melodies [*neumae*] ought to be joyful, [whereas] in sad contexts they ought to be sad"). The latter recalls a phrase in ME, chap. 19 (58.21f.). If *extrinsecus occurrentibus* (translated here as "things outside [the discipline]" refers to matters discussed in the treatise, the phrase probably refers to organum, which is not necessary to the performance of chant and thus is extrinsic to it. For further discussion, see Erickson, "Neoplatonism," pp. 61–3.

4. 62.28–9 Although the meaning of *in praecinendo et respondendo* is unclear, it is as-

D. Explain how these two errors occur.

M. Since the four mutually and suitably different tones make up a harmony,[5] each tone retains its proper quality only when in its proper order and does not give up its place to another. I think you now know the series of tones alluded to.

D. I prefer to entrust all things to your teaching. May I hear you sing these tones?

M. Mark how I sing figure 1.

Thus it is descending.

Thus it is ascending.

Figure 1

From ancient times, names have been assigned to these tones: to the first, that is, lowest tone, the name *protus* or *archous;* to the second, which is a whole tone distant from protus, *deuterus;* to the third, which is a semitone distant from deuterus, *tritus;* to the fourth, which in turn is a whole tone away from tritus, *tetrardus.* Furthermore, they are represented by symbols, as follows: the symbol for the first is a slanted *daseia* sign ⊦ with an *S* at the top: ⨍; [63] that for the second has a *C* turned at the top, thus: ⨍; that for the third is a simple iota, but slanted, thus: ∫; that for the fourth has at the top a *C* lying on its back, thus: ⨍.

D. How does harmony arise from only these four, rather than from a larger number of tones?

M. Obviously, countless tones are used in songs. The number of the tones grows when

---

sumed here that monophonic responsorial or antiphonal performance is implied, and that the error would occur when one singer or group of singers continues where another leaves off, such as at the beginning of the antiphon following a psalm verse. The notion of continuation or succession is implicit in *in praecinendo* at 87.390, where the Master tells the Disciple to imitate his rhythmic performance of fig. 25 (*plaudam pedes ego in praecinendo, tu sequendo imitabere*). On the other hand, P glosses *in praecinendo* with *in cantando* ("in singing [mono-phonically]") and *respondendo* with *organizando* ("singing in organum"), so it is possible—at least to an eleventh-century reader—that *praecinere* meant "to sing the pre-existent melody" and *respondere* "to sing in organum" or "to sing the organal voice (simultaneously with the pre-existent melody)." On *respondere,* see also the note to 25.16.

5. 62.31 (*armonia*). I take *armonia* to be used here in one of the classical Greek senses, namely, as a set of different but agreeably ordered pitches in a *systema* (in this context, the *Enchiriadis* tetrachord).

they follow each other in similarly constituted groups of four, both descending and ascending. Prove this [to yourself] as I sing figure 2.[6]

Figure 2

Therefore, in every harmonious series of tones the melody proceeds both ascending and descending, just as in these tetrachords; and the four sounds, differing amicably among themselves, follow one another in proper succession until they either run out because they are too high or cease sounding because of their lowness. [64] Moreover, each of the four above-mentioned tones asserts control over its tetrachord and likewise its pentachord. Each asserts control over its tetrachord because the four tones are disposed in [their fixed] order in each one of the tetrachords, as in figure 3. Each asserts control over its pentachord in that a tone added above [the tetrachord] is of the same type as was the first, as in figure 4.[7]

Therefore, that which begins and ends with the tone archous ⌐ we call the first pentachord, and it is composed of two whole tones, a semitone, and a whole tone; that which begins and ends with the deuterus tone ℙ we call the second pentachord, and it is composed of three whole tones and a semitone. That which begins and ends with the tritus tone ∫ we call the third pentachord, and it is composed of a semitone and [65] three whole tones; that which begins and ends with the tetrardus tone ℱ we call the fourth pentachord, and it arises from a whole tone, a semitone, and two whole tones.

D. What is a whole tone (*tonus*)?

M. It is a defined distance between two tones, whereby one tone is either higher or lower than another, as between two strings.

6. 63.*descriptio* 2 (fig. 2). Only the four main signs (*notae*) are introduced here. Their other forms are gradually introduced, beginning at 66.107, but without special explanation. All the signs are summarized at the end of the section dealing with "the nature of tones," at 83.340ff. and in fig. 24.

7. 64.75ff. and *descriptio* 4 (fig. 4). Here SE introduces an approach to understanding the tonal system that is not found in ME: scale segments are seen not only in tetrachords (the main constituents of Greek scale systems) but also in pentachords, which are used to illustrate the modular or cyclic structure of the *Enchiriadis* scale. The identity of tones a fifth apart derives from their having the same name, note-form, and quality.

Figure 3

D. What then is a semitone?

M. We call "semitones" or "limmas" those distances between tones that are not of full size. By virtue of their position, they not only impart their properties to the tones but also hold a melody together in sweetness of concord. However, when the semitones are not in their proper place, they make melodies unpleasant. For it is necessary to know that in a series of tones the natural quality exists only when they are a natural distance apart from each other. But if the distance from one tone to another is measured inaccurately, it changes thereupon into another quality and deviates from the original arrangement. This discord results from two errors discussed previously.[8]

D. Would you demonstrate clearly just how such a discord comes about?

M. I shall try as best I can, but pay careful attention. The deuterus tone $\digamma$ is always a semitone below the tritus $\int$; the tritus has the tetrardus $\digamma$ above it; [66] the deuterus[9] $\digamma$ has the protus $\digamma$ below it [figure 5]. You will notice these two phthongi,

8. 65.95 (*supradictis*). The reference seems to be to the second and third errors discussed at 61f.25–9.

9. 66.100. Schmid has, mistakenly, $\digamma$ instead of the $\digamma$ of the sources.

Figure 4

Figure 5

tetrardus f and protus f, in any tetrachord.[10] If, in ascending, the tritus $\int$ is gauged to be immediately after the protus tone f, as if after the deuterus f, one discord will be produced. Likewise, if in descending the deuterus f is gauged to be next after the tetrardus f, as if after the tritus $\int$, another discord will be produced.[11]

10. Either deuterus or tritus is missing from certain tetrachordal series in the examples of errors that follow.

11. 66.102–6 (*Si enim ascendendo . . . haec altera erit absonia.*). In this passage is laid down the two-fold principle underlying the examples that follow: (1) in ascending, the tritus symbol will be used to indicate the semitone above the previous tone, regardless of which tone that is; (2) in descending, the deuterus symbol will be used to indicate the semitone below the previous

D. How is this?

M. Sing the pentachord ascending from the tetrardus ꟼ,[12] calculating so that you will descend by the same steps [as in figure 6].

Figure 6

D. I have sung it.

M. I, too, shall sing the same [pentachord] [figure 7a]. Then I shall add another [pentachord] [figure 7b], where something is shifted from the prior order—namely, at the third step, by measuring out the tritus as if after the deuterus.[13] [67]

Figure 7

Now do you perceive that these two pentachords do not agree with one another?

---

tone (regardless of which tone that is). In the examples, however, no two tones are separated by more than a whole tone. It is important not to identify the daseian symbols with specific pitches here. See also 149.562–4.

12. 66.107. The symbol ꟼ is defined later, at 83.341.

13. 67.*descriptio* 7a/b [figure 7a/b]. In the manuscripts, the illustrations corresponding to figures 7 through 13 of SE are in the form of paired "ladder" (as in Schmid's edition) or trapazoidal diagrams, horizontal lines being used to indicate semitone boundaries. Thus, figure 7a/b is a transcription of a pair of ladder diagrams given by Schmid in the following format:

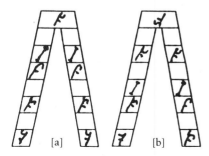

N.B. The tritus sign in the left leg of the second ladder diagram, correct here, is misplaced in Schmid's edition.

Note that in the series of paired melodies beginning with figure 7, the first melody, indicated [a], always represents a legal sequence of pitches and intervals in the daseian scale, whereas the

D. I clearly perceive and understand that the second pentachord [figure 7b] does not return by the arrangement in which it began.

M. So it is: beginning from tetrardus �7, it arrives at archous *ℎ*; this is because on the former side it does not traverse the distance [from archous *ℎ*] to deuterus *ℱ*, but the tone tritus *∫* is measured out through a smaller interval in place of the deuterus. This is signified by a line rather than a box (*paginula*) between [*ℎ* and *∫*].

[68] Sing also the pentachord from protus *ℱ* [as in figure 8].

Figure 8

D. I have sung it.

M. I also shall sing this same thing [figure 9a]; then I shall place the deuterus tone *ℱ* below the tetradus *ℱ* as if it [the tetrardus] were the tritus *∫*, deviating a little from the former order on the latter side [figure 9b].

Figure 9

Did you perceive that the pentachord here deviated from [its normal] arrangement and did not return as it [69] began?

D. Indeed, I did perceive it.

M. Do you see that [the pentachord], having begun with the protus tone *ℎ*, ends with the tetrardus tone �7?

D. I see this indeed.

M. Listen again how, if I violate both sides with these incomplete intervals, [the pentachord] again returns to the tone from which it began [figure 10b]. Let this be the pentachord of the tetrardus �7.[14] Is this clear in your mind?

---

second, indicated [b], always includes one or more tones outside the daseian scale. To aid the reader's understanding of SE's text, some of the daseian symbols used in the manuscript examples are provided above the transcribed melodies where the errors described occur. Regarding the interpretation of the deuterus and tritus symbols in these diagrams and transcriptions, see the note to 66.102–6.

14. 69.*descriptio* 10a. In Schmid's edition the symbol *∫* is twice erroneously positioned.

Figure 10

D. It is certainly clear, both in the illustration for the eyes and in the sound for the ears, that the arrangement differs from one side to the other.

M. It is customary to call these less-than-whole intervals *limmas*. Sometimes through them one mode is changed into another, or the original mode is restored. This can often be [70] observed in chants.

D. We do not regard these things as errors, do we?

M. To be sure, they are errors, but just as barbarisms and solecisms are frequently intermixed in verses for poetic reasons (*figuraliter*), so limmas are sometimes deliberately introduced into chants.

But let us observe still other errors. For a third dissonance, the opposite of the first, comes about, inasmuch as on the first side [of figure 11b] another deuterus is measured from the deuterus *f* as if from protus *f* by an improper distance, that is, one wider than is lawful. Let this therefore again be the pentachord of the tetrardus, with which this species of error is associated.

Figure 11

D. [71] I also understand this discord.

M. Look also at the fourth form of discord of this kind, which is the opposite of the second, that is, when on the second side another tritus is placed after tritus *ſ*, as if from tetrardus *f* [figure 12b]. Let this be the pentachord from the protus *f*.

D. I discern this also because, instead of a deuterus *f* being measured from the tritus *ſ*, another tritus is placed at a greater distance than is fitting after the tritus *ſ*, as if after tetrardus *f*.

M. But if we also add such a pentachord, [72] one that is violated by these errors on

Figure 12

either side, the dissonance will be of this kind. Let this be the pentachord of the tetrardus [as in figure 13].

Figure 13

D. It is indeed a discord, and something that is not sweet-sounding.

M. Since we have comprehended how the distance between two tones can be incorrectly measured, let us also see how this happens: that melodies do not sound in concord with each other if, in those places where it is necessary, tones do not [properly] correspond with other tones.[15]

D. I ask this also.

M. Come here, I say, and see how the arrangement of four-fold variety is disposed in tetrachords and pentachords, so that you will note clearly how far any tone is from another. For just as in colors, if they are ordered in groups of four and put into a series, for example, red, green, yellow, and black, the same color will necessarily be found at every fifth position, with the three [73] other colors in between, so too it happens in tones: while they succeed themselves in every new iteration, [a given tone] is answered by its compeer[16] a fifth away on either side.

15. 72.150 (*soni ad sonos non respondeant*). That is, the tones are not a proper distance from one another. It is possible that an organal context is implied or at least covered by the use of the verb *respondere*. See notes to 25.16 and 62.28f.

16. 73.159 (*compare*). The noun *compar* (English "compeer," "peer," "companion"), which is not found in ME, is another means to designate the identical "quality" (10.6: *suaemet qualitatis*) or "natural kinship" (73.161f.: *naturalis socialitas*) that exists at the interval of the fifth in the *Enchiriadis* scale. Another related term is *sociales* (82.318f.). At 82.320, however, *compar* is associated with the fourth degree.

D. Why do you say they are compeers, when they are different in highness and lowness?

M. Indeed, they are different in highness and lowness. Nevertheless, they are concordant with each other because of a certain natural kinship (*socialitas*). Moreover, each tone has as the second [tone] on this or that side that which it has as the fourth on the other, and any tone has as the third [tone] on one side that which it has as the third on the other. But I say these things insofar as the arrangement of four-fold variety is maintained in the succession of the tetrachords.

D. However, so that I might recognize any given tone, I would like to know the properties of its quality in detail.

M. You ask this for good reason. For, in fact, when the quality of the tones' properties is clear, there is less chance of error in other things. But you will be able to discern these things if you do a simple exercise. Take something to sing that ends, say, on the tone archous *ƒ*. Then something else must be joined to it[17] which [74] begins: [i] from the same tone, or [ii] from its upper or lower compeer [*ϳ* or *Ɣ*], or [iii] from the tetrardus tone *Ƒ*, or [iv] from the tritus tone *ʃ*, or [v] from the deuterus tone *ƒ*.

Therefore, only when that which is joined begins from the tone archous *ƒ* do you make it either [i] equal with the final tone of the melody preceding, that is, precisely the same archous *ƒ*, or [ii] a fifth above or below that tone. However, if [that which is joined] begins from the tetrardus tone *Ƒ*, you put it at either the second below or the fourth above [the archous tone]. If it begins from the tritus tone *ʃ* you put it at either the third below or the third above, but if it begins from the deuterus tone *ƒ*, you put it on either the second above or the fourth below, according to the diagram of the tones given in figure 14, so that what follows [*ƒ*, *ʃ*, or *ƒ*] in no way concords with that which preceded [archous *ƒ*]. The same happens with all the [other] tones [*ƒ*, *ʃ*, and *ƒ*], so that [75] what is added after and what is sung before are unable to be joined in one body of concord if they are mutually joined either above or below [the final or compeer], since the end of one and the beginning of the other each have their own proper position (*mensura propria*), [as in figure 14].

Figure 14

On account of this, where it is proper that this concord be observed it is necessary that the ending and beginning tones be positioned in their respective natural

17. 73.169–76.194 (*Ergo sume aliquid canere . . . ad meli ductum.*). The distance between the last note of one melodic segment and the first note of that immediately following, such as between psalm and antiphon, may produce the third type of discord referred to at 61f.26–9. Simultaneous sounding of tones does not seem to be at issue here: the "leading" or "continuation" of melody (76.194) is the subject at hand.

orders. Where this is disregarded or need not be observed, the things which are sung can proceed in tones concordant in themselves, but those added after are not able to be mutually united in harmony with them. But it ought to be a part of the cantor's expertise to know where one thing after another can be agreeably joined, or where it is not necessary.

Enough has been said concerning such discord (*discrepantia*). It must be known, however, that the first concord [76] is that which is made in the manner mentioned above for the continuation of melody. The second is a slightly lesser concord which occurs when we add [what follows] at the transposition of a fifth above or below,[18] wishing either to ease the difficulty of a high range or to raise that which is too low. There is also a third concord that occurs at the octave, that is, when we change to a new pitch or a higher melody.[19] And a certain agreement can be preserved by these conjunctions of melodies. Otherwise it is not possible, unless perhaps some melody is fundamentally changed by transposition into another mode. If you transpose higher or lower, by an interval of one or two or three tones, a given series of tones making a melody, the category of trope also simultaneously changes into another species.

D. Give an example of this tranposition.

M. Whenever I sing in this way the tetrachords or five pentachords in order, [77] as in figure 15. And so I say that, just as when the pentachord of the first mode, when sung one step higher, is changed into the pentachord of the deuterus, and similarly goes over from the deuterus into the tritus, and from the tritus into the tetrardus, and from the tetrardus it arrives again at the protus, so too, if you completely transpose anything whatsoever higher or lower by one or two or three tones, it will simultaneously be changed into another mode.

For example, this is the customary model melody of the first mode [figure 16].[20] Therefore, if I make the entire arrangement of this model melody higher by one degree, then the deuterus is made out of the protus mode. Likewise, transposed from the deuterus it goes into the tritus mode. In turn, if the melody is raised one step from the tritus tone the tetrardus results. Then, when this is taken higher by

---

18. 76.197 (*transpositione*). As will be clear from context, "transposition" for the author of SE implies shifting a melody from one starting or ending pitch level to another, but not necessarily maintaining the intervallic sequence within the melody. In other words, "transposition" may effect a change of mode.

19. 76.198–9 (*in novam vocem vel acutiorem melos mutamus*). The *nova vox* ("new voice" or "new pitch") an octave higher probably refers to the natural sounding of boys' voices an octave higher than men's, since most melodies cannot be replicated at the octave within the *Enchiriadis* scale. Boys would think within the *Enchiriadis* scale but would naturally produce sounds an octave higher than those represented by the daseian symbols.

20. 77.*descriptio* 16 (fig. 16). This melody and text are used at 82.*descriptio* 23 (fig. 23) and serve as the first part of an example in the *Commemoratio brevis* (158.43; and Bailey, *Intonation Formulas,* pp. 30f.). The melody (minus the fourth tone and with text *Alleluia*) also appears in ME at Schmid pp. 14–9, *descriptiones* 1–6 (fig. 8.1–6), where it is systematically subjected to various transpositions.

Figure 15

No - an - no - - e - a - - ne

Figure 16

one degree the protus is born anew. If these same things were also to be shown by illustrations—as it were, given in visible form—would they not be more evident?

D. [78] Certainly.

M. Therefore, using lines, let us diagram five illustrations that, having a stepwise relation to each other, represent such changes of mode [figure 17].[21] [79] The first illustration is of the protus mode, the second of the deuterus, the third of the tritus, the fourth of the tetrardus, the fifth again of the same as the first. As has been said, whatever melody you transpose in this manner will be turned into another species of mode. If it is of an authentic (*maior*) trope before being shifted, it will also be authentic afterwards, regardless of the mode into which it has been changed. I think you have already learned the number and individual differences of the tropes or modes, which they wrongly call "tones."[22]

21. 78.*descriptio* 17 (fig. 17). This example has a function similar to that of 15.*descriptio* 2 (fig. 8.2) of ME, namely, to show how a melody, when rendered in different modes, has a different internal intervalic succession (as determined by the placement of the semitone).

22. 79.229f. (*Tropi autem vel modi sunt, quos abusive tonos dicunt*). This passage is analo-

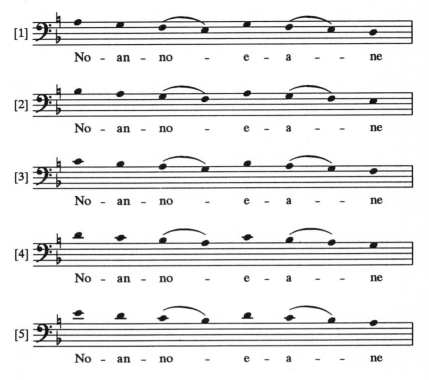

[1] No - an - no - e - a - - ne

[2] No - an - no - e - a - - ne

[3] No - an - no - e - a - - ne

[4] No - an - no - e - a - - ne

[5] No - an - no - e - a - - ne

Figure 17

D. I have learned them, indeed.

M. Sing some melodies in the first mode, also in the second and the others.

D. Here is the first mode. [He sings.] Here is the second. Here is the third. And now the fourth.

M. Tell now, since the ears perceive certain mutual differences between them, what is the cause of this diversity?

D. Indeed, they are perceived to be different from each other by a certain discernible aspect of their properties, but I wonder why this is so.

M. So that it may begin to be clear, sing at least the first tetrachord or pentachord [80] [figure 18].[23]

D. See, I have sung it.

M. For present purposes, use whichever type of the protus you want, and you will

gous to 13.1f. in ME (see corresponding note), except that the inclusion of the term "tropes" better reflects the Boethian model.

23. 80.*descriptiones* 18–22 (figs. 18–22). Note that the diagrams use daseian superiores signs that have not yet been explained. Schmid's notes indicate that many of the oldest manuscripts in fact use the corresponding finales symbols, although those for the superiores tones are given in his edition of the text.

Figure 18

note that all melodies sung according to the protus mode end on the protus tone *Ϝ*.

D. I certainly see this.

M. Sing now another pentachord, one which is one degree higher, beginning and ending on the deuterus tone.

D. That is sung in this way [figure 19].

Figure 19

M. Also sing melodies of the deuterus mode, and compare them with the deuterus tone *Ϝ* to see whether they end on that very same tone.

D. They certainly do.

M. Give now the third pentachord, two degrees higher, which, of course, begins from the tritus tone *⌐* and ends on the same.

D. That is of this kind [figure 20].

Figure 20

M. Compare to this the tritus modes and you will discover that they end on the tritus tone *⌐*.

D. It is definitely so.

M. Now sing the fourth pentachord, three degrees higher, that is, from the tetrardus tone *Ϝ*.

D. That is done in this manner [figure 21].

Figure 21

M. Now look at the tetrardus modes. Do you hear them halting on the tetrardus tone *Ϝ*?

D. I hear it most truly.

M. Now sing the fifth pentachord; the original arrangement of the tones and of the modes now returns in the new tetrachord [figure 22].

Figure 22

D. This, too, is certainly marvelous.

M. [81] Therefore, the character of the four tones controls all melodies. On account of this, now note for yourself the wonderful, varied nature of those four tones and the notation of each, whereby the individual ones mutually differ from one another and accordingly produce the differences of the modes.

D. I do indeed seem to understand these things. Nonetheless, I wonder why you said that with these tones no more than four modes are produced, since it is customary to count eight modes.

M. We are accustomed to counting eight modes, but in such a way that each tone in a tetrachord governs two modes, that is, authentic and plagal; on account of this, those modes that are ruled by the same tone are classed as one mode. That is to say, the protus authentic and plagal modes are ruled by the archous or protus tone ♭; the deuterus authentic and plagal by the deuterus tone ♭; the tritus authentic and plagal by the tritus tone ♪; and the tetrardus authentic and plagal by the tetrardus tone ♭. [82] Appropriately, we call the authentic the principal (*auctoralis*) [and] the plagal the secondary (*subiugalis*) or lateral (*lateralis*) mode. Therefore, not only are the individual tones discernible by their qualitative properties; they all also govern their respective tetrachords and pentachords, and, as has been said, distinguish the "tones" or modes.

D. Therefore, does the character of the final tone alone determine each mode, so that, on account of it, a trope or mode must be said to be of this or that tone (*sonus*) because the end of the melody stops on it?

M. Certainly the nature of any trope is perceived to reside particularly in some final tone; for this reason the trope settles on it upon ending. It must be added, however, that the final tone and its more usual associated tones[24] are found at the ends of commas or colons.[25] Moreover, each tone not only has associated tones at the fifth, but it also seeks those others comparable (*compares*)[26] to itself at the fourth, which is the place of the third symphony.[27] So in phrases that are members

24. 82.318 (*sociales*). The primary reference is to the fifth above the final. Other terms of similar meaning are cited in the note to 73.159.

25. 82.318 (*commatum vel colarum*). For "comma" and "colon" in ME, see especially chapter 9 (22.21ff.).

26. 82.320. The adjective *compar* is here associated with the fourth, not the fifth, degree, although this point is not further developed. See the note to 73.159.

27. 82.321 (*simphoniae*). This is the first occurrence of this term in SE. For "symphony" in ME, see note to 7.14. Discussion of the term in SE is found at the beginning of part 2 (90.1ff.).

of a song, the colons or commas, ascending or descending, nearly always seek out these tones associated with the final, and the melody, whether ascending or descending, seeks to reach them. Properly made melodies give sufficient examples; lest we seek too long, consider that which we have here, a model melody or phrase that is made up of two commas [figure 23].[28]: No ⌣ an ⌐ no ∫ ⌐ e ⌐ a ∫ ⌐ ne ⌐.

No - an - no - - e - a - - ne

Figure 23

[83] See how each comma descends through four tones and how the phrase ends on that tone from which it begins [that is, protus]. On the other hand, what we call "colons" are those larger phrases containing two or three or more commas, which also display certain suitable distinctions (*distinctiones*) among themselves. Furthermore, commas coherently succeeding one another as they rise and fall make up a colon. Sometimes, however, there are places where the terms "colon" or "comma" can be used with equal validity.[29]

D. How do the authentic and plagal modes differ, if both end on and are governed by the same sound?

M. What must be said about these things we shall treat more conveniently if first we describe the proper symbols of the tones. We write signs for eighteen tones, that is, for four and a half tetrachords. We call the first tetrachord, because it is the lower, the *grave*, the second the *finale*, the third the *superius*, the fourth the *excellens*. Appropriately, we designate those tones we call *finales* by their noteforms, which we described above, thus: ⌐ ⌐ ∫ ⌐.

The graves tones, however, are designated by nearly the same signs, but looking backwards, thus: ⅂ ⅂ /\\ ⅂. The superiores tones are designated by the finalis note-forms rotated downwards: ⌡ ⌡ ⅃ ⌡. The excellentes tones are designated by the gravis note-forms rotated downwards: ⌐ ⌐ ⌐ ⌐.

[84] Excepted is the tritus tone, which among the graves has an N slanted /\\, among the superiores N reversed and slanted ⌐, [and] among the excellentes a crossed iota ⌐. We represent the remaining pitches by the supine note-forms ⌐ ⌐. All are put down in order as [labeled in figure 24].

D. How can I tell which tones are finales and which are superiores, or whether they are of one or another arrangement?

M. Everything in music is constituted in relation to something else.[30] For no tone

28. 82.*descriptio* 23 (fig. 23). See note to 77.*descriptio* 16 (fig. 16).

29. 82f.317–33. The grammatical elements of comma and colon are more closely integrated with the theory of the modes here than in the parallel section in ME (22.21ff.). However, both treatments allow that comma and colon are at times indistinguishable.

30. 84.349–50 (*Omne musicum ad aliquid esse constat.*) This notion, which derives from Boethius, is developed further in part 3, 117.37–118.48.

Figure 24

can be a musical one without being joined to another tone in relation to which it sounds musically at a natural distance. Therefore, just as something is not understood in relation to itself (*ad aliquid per se*), so too, if any tones are considered in and of themselves (*absolute*) alone, they cannot rightly be said to be either superiores or finales or as belonging to any specific arrangement. But since whatever is sung correctly, whether higher or lower, concludes on one of these four, it must end on one or another of them. This tone, together with the other tones of its tetrachord, has the name *final,* and from here the other tetrachords assume their arrangement.

Also from this same tone a mode, be it authentic or plagal, receives its ambitus (*mensura*). For since we can put any lower mode a fifth higher and any higher mode a fifth lower, as shown above, it is, therefore, not called higher or lower because the one [85] is sung higher or lower than the other but on the basis of how both modes are constituted in relation to the final tone. However, they are constituted in this way: in a plagal mode the potential range (*potestas*) from the final is equal above and below, that is, it may reach from the final to the fifth tone on either side. This does not always happen, but this is its potential range. Now if it goes beyond the fifth tone in the scale system on the upper side, it is normally classified as an authentic mode. In fact, an authentic mode has in the higher tones a range double [that of a plagal mode], that is, up to the ninth tone.

D. What is a system (*systema*)?

M. We say that intervals (*diastemata*) are in colons and commas, but systems are in more complete phrases (*particulae*) or in an entire period (*periodus*). For an interval is any span of tones by which a phrase is encompassed, that is, is bounded by a higher and a lower pitch. A system is the span of an entire melody. Likewise, the species of tetrachords, [86] pentachords, and octochords are systems that impart their structure (*species*) to the individual modes.

D. Why is one tetrachord positioned below the final tones, whereas two tetrachords are above them?

M. Because, whether sung in a higher or lower register, any simple [that is, monophonic] and legitimate melody descends no lower than the fifth tone below the final tone and ascends no higher than the ninth above [the final].

Since we have finished our discussion of the kinds of errors to be avoided, now we shall with God's help pursue those things which must be discussed regarding the embellishment of melody. In particular, it must be seen that any melody is sung rhythmically.

D. What does it mean to sing rhythmically (*numerose canere*)?

M. To make it understood where one must use longer and shorter durations (*moru-lae*), we shall consider how and to what degree some syllables are short and others long. So let us consider which tones ought to be lengthened and which ought to be shortened, so that those things which [are held] long properly combine with those things which are not, and so that a song is beaten in the manner of metrical feet. Come, let us sing using this exercise. [87] I shall indicate the feet while singing; you, following, will imitate [figure 25].[31]

Figure 25

    Only the last [syllable] in [each of] the three phrases is long; the remaining [syllables] are short. Therefore, to sing rhythmically in this way is to measure durations proper for long and short tones, never extending or contracting here and there more than is proper, but holding out the pitch in conformance with the rule of scansion so that the melody can end in that tempo (*mora*) in which it began. If at different times you wish to change the tempo for the sake of variation, that is, to make the course of the melody around the beginning or end more sustained or more rapid, do it by a factor of two, that is, halve a long duration or double a shorter one.

D. I think it is useful to try these things and put them into practice.

M. You think correctly. Therefore, let us select any melody to sing, now in shorter durations, now in longer durations; hence the durations that were short at one time are lengthened, and the durations that were long at another time are shortened. Let us now sing [figure 26]: [88] the first [line] is in short durations, one in longer lengths follows, then one with short durations again.

    This principle of rhythm is always suitable for properly made song, which in

---

31. 87.*descriptio* 25 (fig. 25). Only two manuscripts—the late-ninth-century Düsseldorf *We* (only a fragment but also the oldest source for SE) and the eleventh century *T*—have prosodic symbols, and even these are incomplete and mutually conflicting. Therefore, both the series of prosodic symbols given by Schmid and the present transcription must be considered hypothetical. This transcription (and presumably Schmid's placement of the prosodic signs) is based on the sentence *Solae in tribus membris ultimae longae, reliquae breves sunt* (87.391), *ultimae* being interpreted as referring to the last syllable of the three phrases, not the last two syllables of these phrases (as in *T*).

E - go sum vi - a ve - ri - tas et vi - ta

al - le - lu - ia al - le - lu - ia

E - go sum vi - a ve - ri - tas et vi - ta

al - le - lu - ia al - le - lu - ia

E - go sum vi - a ve - ri - tas et vi - ta

al - le - lu - ia al - le - lu - ia

Figure 26

its greatest dignity is embellished by it, whether sung slowly or swiftly, whether by one or many singers. It also happens that, as long as in singing rhythmically one does not protract or contract more or less than another, the voice of a multitude is heard as if coming from one mouth. Likewise, in alternating or in answering in the same rhythm, it is important to preserve agreement no less in duration than in pitch.

D. How may songs be concordant through duration?

M. It has been shown above how the harmonious joining of songs occurs when every tone is in its proper place. However, concord of durations comes about if that which must be added answers with equal duration, [89] or, if appropriate, with a duration twice as long or twice as short.

D. It is understood that all the things which have been said above occur in expertly made songs. If there are further things necessary for well-formed melody, proceed.

M. I say that the rule of the distinctions must be observed, that is, that you know what is appropriate to unite and what is appropriate to separate. What tempo is suitable for this or that melody must also be understood. Whereas one melody is better sung more quickly, another is sweeter when sung more slowly. For one can know by the very formation of a melody whether it is composed of fast or slow phrases. Therefore, with clear and sweet melodies you will employ an apt tempo that suits each melody at least by reason of time and place and of any outside condition,[32] and will also [employ] that pitch (*altitudo*) suitable to the tempo. With rules of this kind you will regulate noble and well-constituted music. In addition, an agreeable mixture of symphonies adds very great sweetness to songs.

THE END OF PART 1. THE SECOND PART, CONCERNING THE SYMPHONIES, BEGINS

D. [90] What is a symphony?

M. An agreeable combination of certain pitches. Three of these combinations are simple: diapason, diapente, and diatessaron. Three are composite: disdiapason, diapason-plus-diapente, and diapason-plus-diatessaron.

D. What is the symphony of the diapason?

M. It is sung an octave apart, with six tones (*soni*) in between.

D. What is the diapente and what is the diatessaron?

M. The diapente occurs a fifth apart [and] a diatessaron a fourth apart, just as the outside tones of pentachords and tetrachords accord with each other.

D. Where does the term *diapason* come from?

M. *Diapason* is Greek and in Latin is translated "through all," because the ancient kithara contained only eight strings.

D. Why are the diapente and diatessaron so called?

M. *Diapente* means "through five," because it comprehends five pitches. *Diatessaron* is translated "through four," because it encloses four pitches.

Concerning the diapason and disdiapason

D. How is the diapason sung?

M. When one pitch is changed into another, either descending or ascending, so that the higher and lower [pitches] are not so much consonant as equal-sounding

32. 89.424–5. This second and last use of *extrinsecus occurrens* in SE may indicate that a given melody does not have an intrinsic tempo but is affected by all manner of performance conditions, or it could be a reference to organal performance (see note to 61.14), which is specifically associated with slow tempo (38.14f. and 97.56). However, the final sentence of part 1, beginning with *praeterea* ("in addition," "beyond this"), seems to suggest that the discussion of organum to follow is a brand new topic—something other than *extrinsecus occurrentes*.

(*aequisoni*). With this agreement the harmonizing tones sound the diapason. It is as if, in the following illustration, the pitch were lowered from H to A or raised from H to P [figure 27].[33]

Figure 27

[91] For whether one pitch is taken after the other an octave apart or is sung simultaneously with two equal-sounding pitches, the song of a simple diapason is made by this method. Indeed, we may sing with three pitches simultaneously, as with the three illustrated. [92] In this way the song of a double diapason comes about. Also, if it is sung at the fifteenth with the middle pitch removed, there will be a disdiapason nevertheless. Let us sing all these things according to the manner written out above.

33. 91.*descriptio* 1 (fig. 27). The letters A, H, and P are the first, eighth, and fifteenth letters of the Latin alphabet, and thus indicate octave and double-octave intervals (but not specific phthongi, which are represented by daseian signs in the most reliable sources). The use of letters to label a grid of horizontal lines recalls the diagram at Boethius, *De inst. mus.* 4.14 (Friedlein, p. 341). Since the same sequence of daseian signs is given for all three voices represented, the letters were undoubtedly added to clarify register. However, the inherent problems of representing the doubling voices with a notation that does not allow for all the necessary pitches resulted in a rather chaotic transmission of the illustration. For another use of letters to show octave equivalence, but with a progression from top to bottom, see 27.*descriptio* 4 (ME, fig. 10.4).

Thus, this symphony [the diapason], because it is easier and clearer than the others, is called the greatest and first of the symphonies.

Concerning the diapente

The symphony of the diapente is next. In it either one pitch is taken after the other or both are sung simultaneously a fifth apart, according to the manner written out below [figure 28].[34]

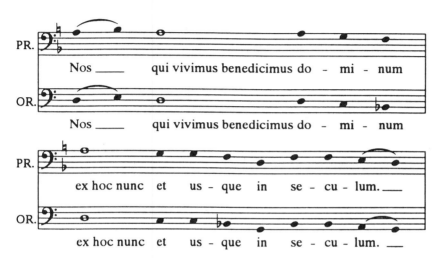

Figure 28

In this manner, therefore, the diapente is sung in its undoubled form (*simpliciter*). However, the first composite form of the diapente occurs if the organal voice is so doubled at the diapason that the principal voice is the middle one, in the same way as the pitch labeled V is between those labeled I and VIII [figure 29]. [93] For I designate the given melody (*absoluta cantio*) the principal voice (*vox principalis*) and that which is added to it by means of a symphony the organal voice (*vox organalis*). Let us now sing according to the manner written out below [figure 29].[35] A second composite form of the diapente occurs when the voice we

34. 92.*descriptio* 2 (fig. 28). This is the only illustration in this series in which the daseian signs are unambiguous and correct. Throughout this series of diagrams the principal voice, since only it is completely confined to the tones of the *Enchiriadis* pitch set, is transcribed on a staff with a mixed "key signature," reflecting the *Enchiriadis* scale's B♭ and b♮.

35. 93.*descriptio* 3 (fig. 29). The musical examples from here through 101.*descriptio* 11 (fig. 37) are riddled with inconsistencies, ambiguities, and errors in the manuscript tradition, primarily with regard to the daseian symbols (eliminated in many of the later manuscripts). The interpretation of the diagrams (which in Schmid's edition preserve some of the problematic elements) is based on these premises: (1) The organal voice below the main principal voice (even when not explicitly given) is labeled I, its octave and double-octave doublings VIII and XV,

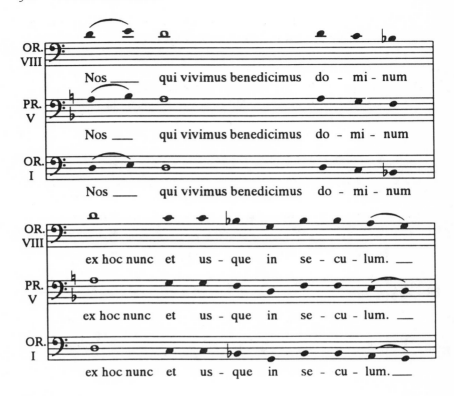

Figure 29

have called principal is so doubled at the diapason that the middle is the organal, as the voice labeled VIII is between those labeled V and XII [figure 30]. Let us sing according to the manner written out. [94] The third composite form of the diapente occurs when the organal voice is doubled at the diapason below the lower principal voice, so that the highest is the principal voice, as that labeled XII is against those labeled VIII and I [figure 31]. This consonance also concords at the twelfth when the middle voice is removed. Likewise, the fourth composite form of the diapente occurs when the principal voice is doubled at the diapason above the higher voice, so that the lowest is the organal voice, as is that labeled I against that labeled V and XII [figure 31]. Similarly, this makes concord also when the middle voice is removed. [95] The fifth composite form of the diapente occurs when it is

---

respectively. (2) Depending on whether the organal interval is a fourth or a fifth, the main principal voice is labelled IIII or V, respectively; it moves in the range $\digamma$ to $\d$ (D to b). Its doubling an octave higher is represented as XI or XII, depending on the organal interval. (3) Only the daseian signs for the main principal voice (i.e., IIII or V) are consistently reliable, even when they are incomplete.

Figure 30

sung with four different voices, with both voices [principal and organal] doubled at the diapason, so that it is clear that those labeled I and VIII correspond[36] as organum[37] to those labeled V and XII. Let all of them be sung according to the manner written out below [figure 31]. [96] The sixth composite form of the diapente occurs when the highest voice is the organal voice, as that labeled XV is to that labeled XII and V, as in the manner written out below [figure 32]. The same symphony can also be varied by means of the multiple type [of ratio],[38] with one or both pitches tripled at the disdiapason. [97]

Concerning the diatessaron

The symphony of the diatessaron is next. It occurs where [tones] are simultaneously sounded a fourth apart. But it must be known that it is not as simple as

36. 95.45 (*respondeant*). On the various translations of *respondere* see note to 25.16.

37. 95.46. This is the first occurrence of the term *organum* in SE.

38. 96.51 (*multiplici specie*). See 119.60–70 (in SE, part 3) for a more formal (if brief) discussion of the category of ratio called multiple.

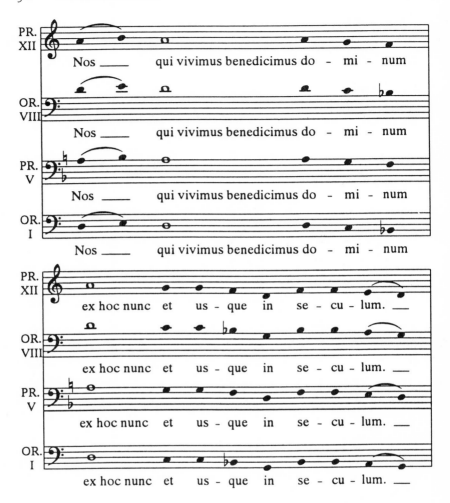

Figure 31

in the other [symphonies], which are larger. Rather the organum is derived from some other natural principle that will be described later. Nevertheless, when it is performed with a moderate slowness, which is most appropriate to it, and with attentiveness to concord, the sweetness of the song will be most becoming [figure 33].

The symphony of the diatessaron is put together in the same ways as the diapente. The first composite form occurs when the organal voice is [98] doubled at the diapason so that the middle voice is the principal voice, as that labeled IIII between those labeled I and VIII, according to the manner written out below [figure 34]. The second composite form occurs when, conversely, the principal voice is so doubled at the diapason that the middle voice is the organal voice,

Figure 32

Figure 33

Figure 34

as that labeled VIII between those labeled IIII and XI [figure 35]. [99] The third composite form of the diatessaron occurs when the organal voice is doubled at the diapason below so that the principal is the highest voice, as that labeled XI is in relation to those labeled VIII and I [figure 36]. Likewise, the fourth composite form of the diatessaron occurs when the principal voice is doubled at the diapason above, so that the organal voice is the lowest, as that labeled I in relation to those labeled IIII and XI [figure 36]. [100] Likewise, the fifth composite form of the diatessaron occurs when both voices—namely, the principal and organal voices—are doubled at the diapason, so that those labeled I and VIII correspond as organum to those labeled IIII and XI [figure 36]. [101] The sixth composite form of the diatessaron occurs when the highest voice is the organal voice, as that labeled XV to XI and IIII. Let this also be sung in the manner written out below [figure 37].

[102] It must be noted that whether the principal voice or the organal voice or both together are doubled at the diapason, a boy's voice can always supply the place of the higher pitch.

D. What is the difference, I ask, between the first composite form of the diapente [figure 29] and the second of the diatessaron [figure 35], since in both cases the

Figure 35

outside pitches are separated from the middle one by an equal interval? Likewise, what is the difference between the second composite form of the diapente [figure 30] and the first of the diatessaron [figure 34]?

M. If you ask why, in the first composite form of the diapente [figure 29], the middle pitch is a principal rather than an organal voice, whereas in the second composite form of the diatessaron [figure 35] the middle voice is an organal rather than a principal voice, since in both cases the same intervals separate the middle voice from the outside voices; and [if you ask] in turn why, in the second composite form of the diapente [figure 30], the middle voice is designated an organal voice, whereas in the first composite form of the diatessaron [figure 34] the middle voice is called a principal voice, you would certainly understand this to be the reason: that at the symphony of the diatessaron an organal voice does not so simply and consistently accompany a principal voice as at the diapente but, by some natural law of its own, it stands still in certain places and is not able to proceed further consonantly. It is also shown in the illustrations cited above how it does not descend below [103] the tone tetrardus γ.

Certainly it must be known from the composite forms previously defined that the diatessaron and diapente also differ by some other property. Indeed, as long

Figure 36

as the tropes or modes always recur at the fifth and at the octave, and as long as the lower voice corresponds with the upper voice at the diapente in the same category of trope, it is necessary that there be at the octave a correspondence again with each voice in the same trope. This is done so that, when the organal voice is doubled at the diapason and the principal voice is the middle voice, the lower organal voice is separated from the middle voice by a fifth and from the upper voice by a fourth, which is the first composite form of the diapente. However, when the principal voice is doubled at the diapason and the organal voice is the middle one, the lower principal voice is separated by a fourth from the middle voice and from the upper by a fifth, which is the second composite form of diapente.

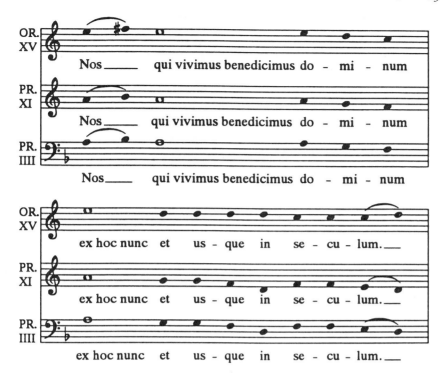

Figure 37

On the other hand, in the diatessaron, since the lower voice does not have correspondence with the higher voice in the same trope a fourth away, it is necessary that the principal voice and the organal voice not correspond to the same trope, but, rather, that each of these voices have its own corresponding trope an octave away. And this is done so that, when the organal voice is doubled at the diapason and the principal voice is in the middle, the lower organal voice is a fourth and the higher is a fifth from the middle, which is the first composite form of the diatessaron. However, when the principal voice is doubled at the diapason and the organal voice is the middle, the lower principal voice is a fifth from the middle voice and the upper is a fourth, [104] which is the second composite form of the diatessaron. The illustrations given above show all these things. What further [would you like to know]?

D. You maintained that at the symphony of the diapente, but not at the diatessaron, the same tropes sound.[39] In the composite form of both these symphonies, the middle voice, although like distances apart from the outside voices, is not of the same trope in both cases: in one case it is [of] the principal [voice], in another

39. See 103.91–105.

the organal. Therefore, I ask, what is the difference between the principal and organal voice of a symphony of the diapente, since they are not dissimilar in [their] tropes?

M. Remember now this rule: When an organal voice at the diapente is doubled, [and] if for the middle—that is, principal—voice there is a like interval [series] in the outside voices,[40] there seems to be no difference between the principal and organal voices. Now, when the lower organal voice is a fifth below the principal voice but is a fourth above it because of the nature of the diapason, just so, conversely, the organal voice is a fourth below the principal voice at the diatessaron but at the diapason is a fifth above [the principal voice]. Similarly, when the principal voice is doubled at the diapason the intervals from the middle voice to the outside voices are not the same. Thus you will easily be able to understand how the character of the symphony of the diapason, which multiplies both voices—both those which are principal and those which are organal—disposes [them] in certain intervals.

D. [105] Why in the symphony of the diatessaron is an organal voice not able to move strictly [in] parallel with a principal voice, as in the other symphonies?

M. Because, as has been said, at a fourth apart tropes are not the same, and melodies of different tropes[41] are unable to proceed simultaneously throughout. This is because at the symphony of the diatessaron the principal voice and the organal voice do not accord harmoniously all the time at the fourth.

D. I would also like to know how at a fourth apart the type of the tropes is different.

M. You will see this easily. For whether it is transposed one tone higher or to the fourth below, a melody of a different trope is discernible if one listens closely. It is sung in the manner written out below [figure 38].

D. I perceive clearly in this transposition that the protus authentic mode goes over into the deuterus authentic. [106] Will you now explain why at some intervals the voices are consonant,[42] whereas in others they are either discordant or not as agreeable?

40. 104.119–20 (*simile intervallum esset ad extremas*). The term *intervallum* here and throughout the paragraph refers to melodic succession rather than vertical distance between tones. The sense of the paragraph is that organum at the fifth allows a melody to be reproduced exactly (that is, the horizontal succession of intervals remains the same) in the organal voice within the Enchiriadis system, whereas this is not consistently the case when the voices are a fourth or an octave apart.

41. 105.132 (*diversorumque troporum modi*). Phrases of the form *modus tropi* or *tropus modi* (seemingly "mode of a trope" or "trope of a mode," respectively) present considerable difficulty to the reader. However, systematic comparison of the uses of *modus* and *tropus* in ME and SE leads to the conclusion that *tropus,* always translated by its cognate "trope," clearly or plausibly refers to an ecclesiastical mode; the one exception is at 156.650, where it is equated with *consonantia.* On the other hand, *modus* has a wide variety of meanings, one of which is "mode" in the musical sense. In this translation, *modus* in the phrases *modus tropi* or *tropus modi* (154.621) is understood to mean "category" or "type."

42. 106.141ff. Phillips *Sources,* p. 271, speaks of this point as dividing the "two layers of Harmonics information" in SE; what preceded was more practical (the "how"); what follows is more theoretical (the "why").

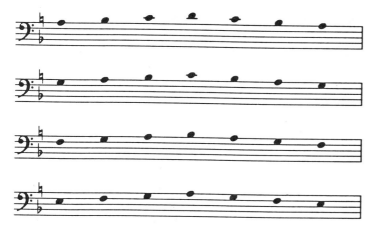

Figure 38

M. Certainly we are permitted to examine the principles the Lord has given by which we may understand somewhat the causes of harmonious and discordant pitches, the nature of the different tropes, and why they migrate through transposition into other species or return again into their own. Just as for counting consistently there is a simple system of numbering, as 1, 2, 3, 4, and so on, which is accessible even to children because of its ease, so the phthongi in music, whose mother is arithmetic,[43] that is, the science of number, are determined in an easy way. And just as the comparison of one thing unequal to another falls into various species of inequality, so [the phthongi], when sung in relation to something else, produce not only the forms of sweet-sounding harmonies but also the sweetest explanations of these very harmonies.

D. How is harmony born of mother arithmetic, and is harmony the same thing as music?

M. Harmony is deemed the agreeable mixture of different pitches; music [that is, the *ars musica*] is the theory [*ratio*] of that agreeableness. Just as music [107] is bound up in every respect with this theory of numbers, as are also the other mathematical disciplines, so it is proper that they be understood through numbers.

D. What are the mathematical disciplines?

M. Arithmetic, geometry, music, astronomy.

D. What is mathematics?

M. Theoretical knowledge.[44]

D. Why theoretical knowledge?

M. Because it deals with abstract quantities.

43. The notion that arithmetic is the mother of music is taken here from Boethius, *De inst. arith.* 1.1 (Friedlein 10.8–10).

44. 107.160–1 From Cassiodorus, *Institutiones* 2.3.6 and 2.3.21 (Mynors 111 and 130). This passage is also found in Isidore, *Etymologiae* 2.24.14–15 and 3:00.1–6, not cited by Schmid.

D. What are abstract quantities?

M. Those things which are without matter, that is, without corporeal mixture, and which are investigated by the intellect alone. In quantities there are multitudes, magnitudes, paucities, smallnesses, forms, equalities, ratios, and so on, "which," to use the words of Boethius, "indeed are incorporeal by their very nature and, existing by reason of immutable substance, are fundamentally altered when joined to something corporeal and are transformed into something ever mutable under the influence of this changeable inconstancy." [45]

Moreover, these quantities are examined in one way in arithmetic, in another in music, in another in geometry, and in another in astronomy. For these four disciplines are not sciences [that is, *artes;* bodies of knowledge] of human invention but modest investigations of divine works; they lead noble minds [to understand] the creation of the world according to the most marvelous principles. Therefore, they cannot be excused who, knowing God and his eternal divinity through these things, [108] have not glorified Him as God and poured forth thanks. [46]

D. What is arithmetic?

M. The discipline treating numerical quantity as such.

D. What is music?

M. The discipline of the theory of pitches that agree and disagree according to numbers, which numbers are in relation to those things found in tones.

D. What is geometry?

M. It is the discipline of fixed magnitude and of forms.

D. What is astronomy?

M. It is the discipline of movable magnitude which, by means of inquiring reason, examines the courses of the stars of the heavens, all the constellations, and the positions of the heavenly bodies relative to each other and to the earth. [47]

D. How are the three other [disciplines] constituted through numerical science?

M. Because all things which are encompassed by these disciplines exist on a basis formed of numbers, and they cannot be understood or described without numbers. For can someone be instructed completely about a triangle or quadrangle or other things that belong to geometry unless he first knows what three or four is? [48]

D. In no way.

M. Can anything be known about the theory of astronomy without number? Whence do we know the rising and setting, the slowing down [109] and the acceleration

45. 107.165–8. From Boethius *De inst. arith.* 1.1 (Friedlein 8.8–11).

46. 107f.172–4. This is derived from St. Paul's Epistle to the Romans 1:21.

47. 108.174–82 (*Arithmetica quid est? . . . circa terram indagabili ratione percurrit*). This passage defining the subjects of the quadrivium is a paraphrase of Cassiodorus, *Institutiones* 2.3.6 and 2.3.21 (Mynors, pp. 111 and 130) and possibly Isidore, *Etymologiae* 3:00.6–11, and is closely related to 107.160f.

48. 108f.185–190 (*Qui enim insinuari potest . . . variationes eius agnoscimus*). Lines 185–7 and 188–90 paraphrase Boethius, *De inst. arith.* 1.1 (Friedlein 11.1–3 and 12.8–10, respectively). A typographical error in Schmid's critical notes gives the starting point of the paraphrase as 108.188.

of the wandering stars? Whence do we learn the period of the moon and its many variations, [and] what part of the zodiac the sun or moon or any other planet may occupy? Is it not so that, just as all these things are done through the certain laws of number, without number they are otherwise unknown?

D. By all means.

M. What principle operates in music so that pitches an octave apart are equal-sounding but those a fifth and fourth apart are consonant? And why again do they correspond as equal-sounding at the fifteenth, but as consonant at the twelfth and eleventh? What indeed are these measures that so aptly join pitches to other pitches so that, if one pitch were somewhat higher or lower with respect to another pitch, they could not concord with each other?

D. It is certainly a wonder, what the commensurabilities[49] of pitches of this kind are. By them the so sweet-sounding symphonies agree with one another, and the remaining tones are so fittingly joined to one another in order. But it is reserved to you to expound upon what you have proposed.

M. I say that at the octave, that is, at the diapason, there is something equal-sounding, because these pitches are related in a duple relationship, as 6 to 12 [or] as 12 to 24. Likewise, [110] those a fifteenth apart are equal-sounding, and this is called the disdiapason because [the pitches] stand in the quadruple proportion, as 6 to 24. At the fifth, which is the diapente, they are consonant with each other because they are in the sesquialter ratio. But the sesquialter is that in which the lesser [term] contains two parts and the greater three, as 6 to 9 or as 8 to 12. Likewise, pitches a fourth apart, which is the diatessaron, are consonant because they are in the epitritus [4:3] ratio. Epitritus or sesquitertian, however, is a ratio in which the lesser [term] has three parts and the greater four, as 6 is to 8 or as 9 is to 12. For this reason they produce concord when combined at the twelfth, because the diapente answers the diapason, that is, the sesquialter [answers] the duple, as 18 to 12 and 6, or as 8 to 12 and 24, or because at the twelfth triples are made, as 18 to 6 or as 24 to 8. For this reason also [pitches] are consonant at the eleventh, because the diatessaron answers the diapason, that is, the epitritus [answers] the duple, as 16 to 12 and 6, or as 9 to 12 and 24. Therefore, the pitches which constitute the symphonies mentioned above—namely, the diatessaron, [which] passes through four tones, and the diapente, which passes through five—concord by means of this relationship, [111] specifically by the epogdous, that is, the sesquioctave, by which diatessaron and diapente are connected to each other. For the difference between a sesquialter and a sesquitertian is always the epogdous. Indeed, in this

49. 109.198–9 (*commensurabilitates*). Here first occurs an important term, more fully discussed in part 3, 125ff.162–267, especially 126.176–92. *Commensurabilis* is found in Boethius—indeed, Boethius, *De inst. arith.* 1.18 (Friedlein 37.19–39.15) is devoted to it—but the term is used only once in the *De inst. mus.* (1.31 [Friedlein 222.9]). The much greater emphasis on the term in SE is probably explainable by the fact that commensurable ratios, i.e., multiples and superparticulars, are those underlying the intervals used in organum. ME, lacking any formal exposition of number theory, does not discuss commensurability.

proportion are 8 to 9, 16 to 18, 32 to 36, and so on to infinity [figure 39]. [Here follows] an illustration of the things that are described.

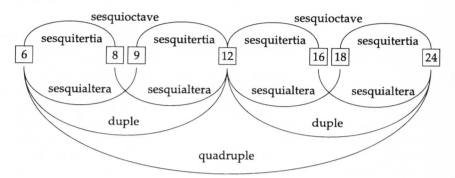

Figure 39

[112] Moreover, the symphonies at the diapason and disdiapason are more perfect than those at the diatessaron and diapente, because the former are of multiple inequality, the latter of superparticular inequality. For multiple inequality is more perfect than superparticular inequality.

It is evident, for this reason, that pitches in the proportions cited above, that is, duple, triple, quadruple, sesquialter, sesquitertian, [and] sesquioctave, constitute consonances or equal-sounding [intervals], because certainly only these related numbers are commensurate and reckoned with in all the disciplines. On account of this they are applied to the symphonies and the remaining musical pitches. Indeed, precise (*modulatae*) pitches are generated through these numbers. Therefore, do you not perceive that music can be explained only on the basis of the principles of arithmetic?

D. I understand clearly that arithmetic is indispensable for a knowledge of music.

M. Absolutely indispensable, since music is formed completely according to the model of numbers. And truly, if you take two strings or two pipes equal in width, and make one double in length, as 12 to 6 or 24 to 12, they will sound the diapason together. If you measure out a string, or a pipe of equal length, [that is] longer by a third than a shorter one, as 8 to 6 or as 16 to 12, or if you make it shorter by a fourth part of the larger, as 9 to 12 or as 18 to 24, there will indeed be [produced] the consonance of the diatessaron, [113] as 8 to 6 and 16 to 12, and similarly 9 to 12 and 18 to 24. In turn, 9 to 6 and 8 to 12, and likewise 18 to 12 and 16 to 24 will be the diapente.

It happens in this way. Just as there is contained within the duple the sesquialter and sesquitertian, so 8 and 9 are contained between 6 and 12, and 16 and 18 are contained between 12 and 24. Alternately, it is evident that that which is the sesquialter to the smaller number, as 9 to 6 and 18 to 12, makes a subsesquitertian to the larger, as 9 to 12 or as 18 to 24. And in turn that which is the sesquitertian to the smaller, as 8 to 6 or as 16 to 12, is the subsesquialter to the larger, as 8 to 12 or as 16 to 24. Thus, between two tones sounding the diapason together, nature has disposed the symphonies at the fourth and fifth so that that which is the diatessaron at the fourth on one side is the diapente at the fifth on the other side, and that which sounds the diatessaron to that side at the fourth sounds the diapente to this [side]. Furthermore, 9 surpasses 8 in the sesquioctave proportion, as also 18 [exceeds] 16 and 36 [exceeds] 32. Thus, if a larger pipe or string exceeds the lesser by an eighth part, they sound together a whole tone.

Therefore,[50] number controls through the proper measurements of pitches whatever is agreeable in well-formed melody. Whatever is admirable in a delightful rhythm or in well-formed melodies or in any rhythmic movements [114] is all produced by number. Pitches certainly pass away quickly; numbers, however, which are altered through the corporeality of voices and the material substance of things in motion, remain. Therefore, as St. Augustine said,[51] reason—which understood that numbers ruled and perfected everything in rhythms, in Latin called numbers, or in well-formed melody itself—investigated [numbers] very diligently and perceived them to be divine and eternal. Next, this same reason, contemplating heaven and earth discerned that beauty alone was pleasing to it, and so also shapes in beauty, dimensions in shapes, and numbers in dimensions. These things, properly divided and arranged, [reason] brought together into a discipline which it called geometry. The motion of heaven also much excited it, and it was moved to contemplate it diligently. Also here, because of the very constant alternation of the seasons and the calculated and defined paths of the planets through the regulated spaces of the intervals [between them], it [reason] understood that nothing other than measure and proportions dominated. Likewise, organizing these things by defining and distinguishing them, it produced astrology.

In this way all things that have to do with proportionality are met in the mathe-

---

50. 113.259–84. Phillips *Sources*, p. 154, has identified the immediate source for the passage beginning here as the "Augustine-Cassiodorus florilegium," which exists in several ninth-century copies (described in Phillips *Sources*, p. 539). It contains the complete *Institutiones* of Cassiodorus (with interpolations from Boethius, *De inst. arith.*), followed by excerpts on the liberal arts from various writings of Augustine.

51. Schmid 114.263–4 (*ut ait sanctus Augustinus*). This introduces a condensation of Augustine's *De Ordine* 2.14f.41–3. At 2.6.26, Augustine had taught that the wise acquire knowledge by the two-fold path of authority and reason. Authority provides the first access to the necessary truths for ordering one's life. Reason, however, is a (human) mental faculty by which things are seen to be connected or separated (2.6.30). Reason is what differentiates man from beast and offers the very capable a means to knowledge of God and of the human and world souls. Augustine had explained how, through the force of reason, the sciences and arts of language—grammar, logic, and rhetoric—had been born; and then (2.14.39) how reason, seeking to contemplate the divine, had sought to build a graded, orderly way to this end using the arts already developed. Following a description of how reason had ordered sounds to produce poets and poetry, there begins the passage paraphrased in SE, which describes the invention of the mathematical arts through the agency of reason.

matical disciplines. Those that are perceived are rather [like] shadows and images of the eternal numbers, which are contemplated by thinking and by reflecting. [115] Therefore, who would say that the basis of numbers is changeable or that any art does not arise through this?

D. Now it is sufficiently clear that not only music but also the other three disciplines are founded on the teaching of numbers. But I pray you to undertake to treat more fully the nature of numbers and to repeat certain things that have been said before, so that by reflecting on them I may somehow arrive at the inner secret of the basis of music by means of the authority of numbers.

THE END OF THE SECOND PART.
HERE BEGINS THE THIRD PART

D. I ask in particular that you explain what *quantity* is.[52]

M. We speak of quantity both in numbers and in masses. Numerical quantity, properly speaking, is called *multitude,* which is accumulated in units. Spatial quantity, which is found in masses, is called *magnitude,* which is divisible into units. Multitude grows by unlimited addition. Magnitude diminishes by unlimited division. That is, a multitude, growing by adding many to one, increases in size; a magnitude, going from one to many, is diminished by the size of its units. [116] Take, for example, a stone or a tree: the smaller the number by which it is divided, the greater the size of the parts; but when they are divided into many parts, their size is thereby made smaller. Thus, for example, a half of 24 is 12, a third is 8, a fourth is 6. Similarly, a half of 12 is 6, a third is 4, a fourth is 3.

In likeness to both kinds of quantity, arithmetic brings forth out of itself music, and in a wonderful way through the contrary qualities of both kinds [of quantity] it disposes pleasant-sounding tones in smooth concordance. Therefore, when the ratio between two pitches is duple, triple, or quadruple—which produces the diapason, diapason-plus-diapente, and disdiapason, respectively—this relationship preserves the nature of *numerical* quantity. However, when the larger number exceeds the smaller by half of the smaller, by a third, or by a fourth, or by an eighth part—which sounds the diapente, diatessaron, and whole tone—this resembles *continuous* quantity.[53] Therefore, when the differences of pitches are based on quantity in this way, the pitches sound together in a sweet mixture according to the contrary natures of the two types of quantity [figure 40].[54]

---

52. 115ff.1–39. The opening discussion of quantity recalls immediately Boethius, *De inst. arith.* 1.1 (Friedlein 7.20–12.12), which is summarized in Boethius, *De inst. mus.* 2.3 (Friedlein 228f.). There are, however, no extended literal borrowings.

53. For the notion of continuous quantity, see Boethius, *De inst. mus.* 1.6 (Friedlein 193.15).

54. 116.*descriptio 1* (fig. 40). This diagram is based on Boethius, *De inst. mus.* 2.20 (Friedlein 251), but it also bears some similarity to other triangular and "lambda" diagrams found in Calcidius (Waszink, pp. 82, 90, and 98). On the ranking of consonances, see also note to

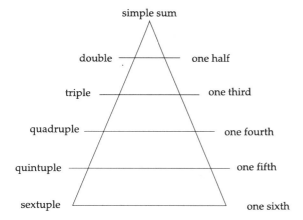

Figure 40

D. [117] If these things are now clear, let us pursue what remains.

M. Certainly it is clear that the first type [of relationship] is assigned to numerical quantity, because the increases grow by the order of the numbers. However, the second type is consistent with continuous quantity, because it decreases in like manner by diminutions, following the order of the numbers. For just as the former exceeds by double, so the latter compresses to a simple half. Just as the former grows three-fold or four-fold, so conversely the latter is more easily made into a third or fourth part.

D. It remains for you to describe how and in what order a concord of tones is determined through these two types of quantities.

M. In explaining with God's help a few things about these matters, as we proposed, let us put first the nature of numbers. We have said that there are two species of quantity, multitude and magnitude. Now, some things having multitude or magnitude are immobile, others movable. Some things exist in terms of themselves (*per se*), as a people, a chorus, a mountain, one thousand, two thousand, three thousand. Other things exist not in terms of themselves but in relation to something else (*ad aliud*), like duple, triple, or quadruple. Geometry treats immobile quantities, whereas astronomy examines movable quantities. And arithmetic examines that which is quantified in terms of itself. But [118] let us consider that [quantity] which is in relation to something else (*ad aliquid*), because through it harmonic sweetness is governed by divine providence.

132.295. *Sescuplus* here (as at Schmid 129.234f.) is the multiple 6, as in Boethius, *De inst. arith.* 2.44 (Friedlein 147.8). However, the term is also used in a non-Boethian way for the ratio 3 : 2. This occurs once in ME (*sescupla*, 21.9) and many times (also in the form *sescuplaris*) in SE, beginning at 124.151. Phillips *Sources*, pp. 275 and 372f., proposes Censorinus 10.11 as the source for ME and Calcidius (for example, at Waszink 84.13–16) for SE.

All number and whatever is expressed in number either exists by itself (*per se*) or is spoken of in terms of some relationship.[55] A number said to be without relationship, as 1, 2, 3, 4, and so on, exists by itself. Furthermore, whatever is spoken of as being relative is either equal or unequal [to something else]. That which is equal, when compared to something, is neither lesser nor greater in sum, as 10 to 10, or 3 to 3, or cubit to cubit, or foot to foot, and things similar to these. It is well known that this category of quantity related to something,[56] that is, equality, is naturally indivisible. For no one can say that [of two equal things] one has one kind of equality but the other has another.[57]

D. Certainly, for what other species [of equality] can there be, wherein one thing is the same as another?

M. But notice what the classes of unequal relationship are. First, it [inequality] is split into greater and lesser (*maior* and *minor*).[58] Then there are five species of greater.[59] The first is called multiple, the second superparticular, the third [119] superpartient, the fourth multiple superparticular, [and] the fifth multiple superpartient. To these five divisions of greater inequality are opposed respectively five divisions of lesser [inequality]; hence they are designated with the same names, distinguished only by the prefix *sub-*. They are called submultiple, subsuperparticular, subsuperpartient, multiple subsuperparticular, and multiple subsuperpartient. Now let us examine both of these classes of inequality, which are separate.

55. 118.39–40. This and the next sentence are paraphrased from Cassiodorus, *Institutiones* 2.4.5 (Mynors 135.16–136.1), not 2.3.5 as in Schmid's critical notes. The material and vocabulary that follow in SE seem at first glance to continue the paraphrase, but see note to 118.42–8. In fact this is an illuminating example of how excerpts from different sources are woven together to provide a continuous narrative.

56. 118.45–6 (*Hanc autem partem relatae ad aliquid quantitatis*). There are other categories of "quality related to something" besides equality.

57. 118.42–8 (*aut aequale est . . . huiusmodi*). This passage is taken virtually verbatim from Boethius, *De inst. arith.* 1.21 (Friedlein 45.12–20).

58. 118.51 (*maius atque minus*). The dichotomy of "greater and lesser" inequalities is found in both Boethius, *De inst. arith.* 1.21f. (Friedlein 45.26–46.17) and Cassiodorus, *Institutiones* 2.4.5 (Mynors, 135, diagram; 136.11,15 [lacuna], 137.8). On the other hand, in the exposition of the various types of inequality that follows, SE neither adopts the Boethian terms *duces* and *comites* (see *De inst. arith.* 1.24 [Friedlein 49.27–50.7]) as synonyms for *maior* and *minor*, nor borrows the manner of Cassiodorus, *Institutiones* 2.4.5 (Mynors pp. 136–8) in defining numbers designated multiple, submultiple, etc., adhering instead to the more Boethian style of speaking of multiple and other "species" or "forms" of inequality.

59. 118f.52–8 (*Est enim una . . . multiplex sub-superpartiens*). This passage naming all the species of proportion is a modified quotation from Boethius, *De inst. arith.* 1.22 (Friedlein 46.6–16). The same content is given diagramatically in Cassiodorus, *Institutiones* 2.4.5 (Mynors p. 135).

Concerning multiple inequality

Inequality is *multiple* when the larger number contains the lesser two, three, four, or more times.[60] And so 2 when compared to 1 is duple, 3 to 1 triple, 4 to 1 quadruple, and so forth. There follows the *submultiple*, namely, that which has the multiple below—2, 3, 4, or more. For example, 1 is contained two times in 2, and this is called subduple; 1 is contained three times in 3, and this is called subtriple; 1 is contained four times in 4, and this is called subquadruple; and so for the rest of this class, which, as you know, we discussed briefly above.[61] [120]

Concerning the superparticular

M.[62] Observe also another [species of] inequality within that [the greater] category of quantity. Here, in contrast [to multiple quantity], the larger part decreases to infinity. This is the [species of inequality] which is called *superparticular*. In it, when two numbers are compared, the first contains the entire smaller number plus some part of it. If this part is half the smaller, it is called sesquialter [3:2]; if a third part, it is called sesquitertian [4:3]; if a fourth, it is called sesquiquartan [5:4]; and if a fifth, it is called sesquiquintal [6:5]; and in this manner the names will tend toward infinity, as the forms of the superparticular progress to infinity. The lesser [forms of the superparticular, that is, the subsuperparticular], which complement [the greater ones], are also made up of whole numbers plus some part of them. One is called subsesquialter [2:3], another subsesquitertian [3:4], another subsesquiquartan [4:5], another subsesquiquintal [5:6], and similarly, proceeding according to the pattern and size of the larger ones. Thus you are now sufficiently able to distinguish this category [of inequality] from the former one.

D. I certainly recognize that, unlike in the first category, the lesser number contains the whole quantity of the larger number except for some part: whether half, as in 2:3, 6:9, and 12:18; or a third, as in 6:8, 9:12, and 12:16; or a quarter, as in 4:5, 8:10, and 12:15. But with respect to the lesser part [of a whole], [121] a half part is greater than a third, a third greater than a fourth, a fourth greater than a fifth, and thus a part named from a greater number itself decreases unendingly.

Concerning the superpartient

M. Consider also the third species of inequality, called *superpartient*. It occurs where a number compared to another contains in itself the entire smaller number plus

---

60. 119.60–5 (*Multiplex . . . aut quater*). This is taken almost verbatim from Cassiodorus, *Institutiones* 2.4.5 (Mynors 136.16–22), the principal difference being that SE uses the Boethian form *multiplex inequalitas* (for Cassiodorus's *multiplex numerus*) and the Boethian names of the submultiple forms.

61. 119.70 (*supra dictum est*). At 117.22–8 relationships later defined as multiple and submultiple are assigned to numerical and continuous quantities, respectively.

62. 120.71ff. This section through Schmid 120.82, except for the first three sentences of the translation (120.71–3), is taken directly from the opening of Boethius, *De inst. arith.* 1.24 (Friedlein 49.15–26).

other parts of it—two, three, four, five, or however many.[63] For example, when 3 is contained in 5 with another two parts, it is called superbipartient [5:3]; when 4 is contained in 7 plus three parts, it is called supertripartient [7:4]; when 5 is contained in 9 plus four parts, it is called superquadripartient [9:5]; and so on. The lesser species that is inferred from the greater is called *subsuperpartient* [for example, 3:5 or subsuperbipartient]. These remarks should suffice concerning this species of inequality.

D. I think they do suffice.

Concerning the multiple superparticular

M. After the three simple species [of inequality] follow two which are made up of the preceding ones. The first of these is called the *multiple superparticular,* which arises out of both [categories of inequality], as 2 to 5, 3 to 7, 4 to 9, or 5 to 11.[64] Because one number contains [the other] more than once it is of the multiple [category]; because [the larger number] exceeds the lesser by a fraction it is of the superparticular category. Therefore, that which is double another number plus its half is called duple sesquialter [5:2]; [122] that which is double the other number plus a third of it is called duple sesquitertian [7:3]; that which is double the other number plus a fourth [is called] duple sesquiquartan [9:4]; and so on. If it is three times [another number] plus its half, or plus a third, or plus a fourth, it is called triple sesquialter [7:2], triple sesquitertian [10:3], triple sesquiquartan [13:4], and so on. That may be enough concerning this inequality, too.

D. Indeed, it is enough.

Concerning the multiple superpartient

M. The fifth inequality is that called *multiple superpartient.* It occurs whenever one number compared with another contains the whole of the other number more than once, plus an additional two or three or however many parts [of it], according to the species of superpartient ratio. These are named after their particular fractions: thus duple superbipartient, as 8 to 3, [where the larger number] contains 3 two times plus two-thirds [of the smaller number], as is also the case with 16 to 6. Similarly for duple supertripartient [such as 11:4] and duple superquadripartient [10:3], triple superbipartient [11:3], triple supertripartient [15:4], and triple superquadripartient [19:5].

Therefore, whatever in the world compares unequally to something else, [or] whatever quantity compares unequally to [another] quantity, corresponds to one

---

63. 121.91–6 (*quae fit . . . quattuor partibus suis*). This passage, clearly based on Cassiodorus, *Institutiones* 2.4.5 (Mynors, 137.17–21)—not 2.3.5 as in Schmid's critical notes—also corresponds closely to Boethius, *De inst. arith.* 1.28 (Friedlein 57.11–4).

64. 121f.100–11. The first sentence of the description of the multiple superparticular is a free paraphrase of the opening of Boethius, *De inst. arith.* 1.29 (Friedlein, 60.19ff.), which, however, does not give any numerical examples. The balance of the description is taken almost word for word from the same chapter (Friedlein 61.8–10 and 17–24, respectively).

of these inequalities. Certainly it is established that multiple [123] inequality, as has been said,[65] pertains to numerical quantity; spatial quantity, however, pertains to the remaining four inequalities. Likewise, musical pitches, that is, those coming together in sweet concord, are expressed variously according to the multiple and superparticular categories. Discordant pitches, on the other hand, imitate the remaining inequalities. Since there is an uncountable and infinite variety of such inequalities, an infinite number of discords follows from this infinitely varied inequality. Only the two [categories of ratio] of which we spoke first pertain to music; the three remaining stand apart from music.

D. Therefore, in what way are only these two associated with music?

M. Because every harmonious accord of the phthongi is formed according to these ratios (*numeri*), which are either multiple or superparticular. Wherever pitches are inconsonant, they are related according to the remaining inequalities.

D. By what principle do pitches, consonant or inconsonant, imitate one ratio or another?

M. Just as different tones agree with each other, so do they differ according to their inequalities.

D. Wherein lies this difference?

M. In highness and [124] lowness, in rising and falling.

D. How do they differ among themselves in relation to the ratios cited earlier, and how do they agree while differing?

M. All phthongi, that is, tones compatible with one another, are distant from one another by duple, triple, or quadruple intervals, which are species of multiple inequality; or by sesquialter, sesquitertian, or sesquioctaval intervals, which are species of superparticular inequality. This interval between phthongi is not one of silence but of the space by which one exceeds the other.

D. Which phthongi are separated by the duple [interval]?

M. Always any [that are] eight steps apart; this is called the diapason.[66]

D. Which are separated by the triple?

M. Always those [that are] twelve steps apart; this is called the diapason-plus-diapente.

D. Which are separated by the quadruple?

M. Always all those [that are] fifteen steps apart; this is called the disdiapason.

D. Which phthongi are of the sescuple species?

M. Always those five steps apart; this is called the diapente.

D. Which are of the sesquitertian species?

M. Those separated by four steps; this is called the diatessaron.

D. Which phthongi have the sesquioctave interval?

M. Any two tones separated [by the interval] called the whole tone, as between two

---

65. 123.125 (*ut dictum est*). At 116.14–7.

66. 124.146–8 (*Qui ptongi duplo . . . dicitur*). From this exchange it is clear that the discussion concerns the Greater Perfect System rather than the daseian system described earlier in the treatise, since the latter does not "always" (*semper*) produce the diapason at the eighth step.

[adjacent] strings. Also, to these intervals is added the semitone, which is not the full interval of a whole tone. [125] By these dispositions of the intervals, divine nature has ordained the harmonious diversity of the tones; by them harmonic sweetness is governed. Whatever sounds above or below what the measures of these proportions demand falls into one or another of the species of the remaining inequalities and is discordant and unsuitable for song.

D. How are the phthongi of music known to have the measures given above, when [the measures] are perceivable neither by sight nor by touch?

M. First, it is known from this: that only these forms of ratios, that is, the multiple and superparticular, are mutually connumerate, and in a certain way commensurate [ratios] are related by their commensurality.[67] For there is nothing in the world, [whether] in solid bodies or in the powers [of the elements],[68] that is joined together compatibly without being linked through this fraternal kinship of the proportions. These proportions are the only ones in which meters combine together concordantly, using different feet. For their joinable nature has so much strength that the very contrary powers of the four elements are united by the agency of these proportions, as is revealed in the *Timaeus* and other philosophers.[69] Hence it follows:

You join the elements through number, so that cold things accord with flames, dry things with liquids.[70]

On account of this, [126] musical tones will not come together so sweetly in one well-formed arrangement of tones unless the commensurality of the proportions unites them through the congruent and consonant intervals discussed above.

D. What is a *commensurable* or *connumerable* [relationship]?

67. 125.164–6 (*connumeratae . . . et commensuratae suaque commensuralitate*). At 109.198f. and at 112.232 there are passing references to commensurability and connumeration. Now these related concepts will be treated in detail to explain how it is that only multiple and superparticular ratios underlie the consonances of music and, indeed, every level of cosmic order.

68. 125.167 (*in potentiis*). *Potentia* is here equivalent to *vis*, *virtus*, and *potestas* (see note to 5.34–7) but in reference to the elements. A parallel usage is in Boethius, *De inst. mus.* 1.2 (Friedlein 188.6–10): "*Iam vero quattuor elementorum diversitates contrariesque potentias nisi quaedam armonia coniugerat, qui fieri posset, ut in unum corpus ac machinam convenirent?* [For now what could make the diversity and contrary natures of the four elements such that they come together in one body and mechanism, unless they are joined by a certain harmony?]" Furthermore, a gloss on *potentiis* in the eleventh-century *Do* reads: "Namely, the elements."

69. 125.171 (*sicut in Timeo*). This is a metonymical reference to Plato, whose *Timaeus* was virtually the only work of that philosopher known to the ninth century and that mainly through the translation and commentary by Calcidius, which is quoted in ME and was apparently also known to the author of SE. See note to 116.*descriptio 1*.

70. 125.172f. The quotation is from Boethius, *Consolatio philosophiae* 3.9b.10f., trans. S. J. Tester in *Boethius: The Theological Tractates* (Cambridge: Harvard University Press, 1973), p. 273. The translation here is mine, however.

M. Where there is a certain common measure between greater and smaller, as 2 to 4, 2 to 6, or 2 to 8.[71] Is not 2 taken twice in the number 4, three times in the number 6, [and] four times in the number 8?

D. Indeed.

M. Therefore, however many times you multiply this simple sum in this way, that many times will the larger sum include this simple sum, so that 3 doubled gives the number 6, tripled the number 9, quadrupled the number 12, and so on. Indeed, what [is it that] occurs in the superparticular [ratios], such as 4 to 6, but that the number 2 is contained in the smaller twice and in the larger three times, which is the sescuple? Likewise in 6 to 8, which is the epitritus: is not the number 2 contained in the smaller three times and in the larger four times? Likewise in 8 to 10, which is the sesquiquartal: is not 2 contained in the smaller four times and the larger five? Thus it goes into infinity: by whatever part a larger number exceeds [a smaller], both are mutually measurable by the whole part, just as 9 exceeds 8 by its eighth part, that is, by a unit, and this same unit, by which they differ from each other, is contained in both. Now you understand how these inequalities control increase or reduction through any common measure.

D. I understand now why they are called commensural or connumeral, but explain how this same [127] connumeration or commensuration is lacking in the other inequalities.

M. Let us ponder this, as you request. Take 3 to 5, which is the superbipartient ratio, and see by what fraction of 3 the 5 is larger.

D. I do not see how I could assent that it is larger by the whole or by one part.

M. In fact, it is not possible. For in this category [of ratio] the smaller is not evenly contained in the larger, as in the multiple [ratio], nor is there any one part that is the difference between the two, as in the superparticular. For in the sesqialter proportion, such as 4 to 6, the number 2, which is the difference between them, is evenly contained in both. Also in the sesquitertian proportion, such as 6 to 8, the number 2, which is the difference between them, is evenly contained in both. But in the superpartient proportion, such as 3 to 5, the number 2, which is the difference, is not evenly contained in either. The same thing also occurs in the multiple superparticular, as 2 to 5, which is the duple sesqialter; as 2 to 7, which is the triple sesqialter; [and] as 3 to 7, which is the duple sesquitertian. The same also happens in the multiple superpartient, as 3 to 8, which is the duple superbipartient;[72] as 3 to 11, which is the triple superbipartient, [and] as 4 to 11, which is the duple supertripartient.

71. 126f.177–209 (II ad IIII . . . IIII ad XI). Inexplicably, ratios are expressed here in their "lesser" numerical forms, i.e., with the smaller term first, although the name of the "greater" form is used. Hence 3 to 5 is incorrectly called superbipartient rather than subsuperbipartient (127.195). In neither the De inst. arith. nor the De inst. mus. of Boethius are the "lesser" forms (minores, comites) of ratios expressed explicitly in numerical terms.

72. 127.208 (III ad VIII, qui est duplex superbipartiens). Here the 8:3 ratio is unequivocably assigned to the ratios lacking commensurability; hence its corresponding interval, the eleventh [used in organum], is a dissonance. This contradicts the beginning of SE, part 2, where

You see, then, that proportions of this kind are not evenly measured either by a simple quantity or by their differences, nor are they augmented by the fractions by which [128] they differ, nor can they be reduced to these [fractions], and for this reason they are called with good reason incommensurate and inconnumerate. On the other hand, just as we perceive both crooked and straight things with our eyes, and indeed anything lying within our vision, so do pitches bound together by means of these commensural intervals delight the hearing, since our nature is constituted in agreement with the ratios mentioned above.[73] The others, however, are dissonances. But do you want to know more about this commensurality?

D. It is up to you to judge this.

M. We have explained how multiple ratios are measured by their quantity and superparticular ratios by their differences. Now let us see what relationship these same multiple ratios have with the superparticular. Set down the fixed order of the multiple ratio; at the same time that of the superparticular is constructed. Both series may be either in their fundamental terms, which have the difference 1 between them,[74] and which are the roots of multiple and superparticular ratios; or they may be in larger numbers derived from these fundamental terms by multiplication. The fundamental terms are 1, 2, 3, [and] 4; and the number 4 fully includes all the symphonies. For 2 to 1 is duple, which is the diapason; 3 to 1 is triple, which is the diapason-plus-diapente; 4 to 1 is quadruple, which is the disdiapason; 3 to 2 is sesquialter, which is the diapente; [and] 4 to 3 is sesquitertian, which is the diatessaron. The derived terms are 6, 12, 18, 24, and so on [129]. For 12 to 6 is duple, 18 to 6 triple, and 24 to 6 quadruple. Moreover, triple to duple is sesquialter, quadruple to triple sesquitertian. Likewise, quincuple to quadruple is sesquiquartan, sescuple to quincuple is sesquiquintal, [and] septuple to sescuple is sesquisextal. Thus the superparticulars accompany the multiples to infinity, so that music is not unjustly said to be generated simultaneously out of both.

D. It is clear without doubt that both connumeration and the relationship of numbers of this kind exist.

M. Therefore, because it is evident how the multiple [ratios], arranged in order, are superparticular to their very selves, so also it may be evident to you how the multiples of the duple or quadruple are composed from the superparticular— [specifically] the sesquialter and sesquitertian. For when we begin from the number 6, let the sesquialter to 6 increase the number to make 9. Let the sesquitertian to 9 increase the number to make 12. And thus the duple, the ratio 12 to 6, is completed by the sesquialter and sesquitertian. Likewise let the sesquialter to the

---

the diapason-plus-diatessaron is given as a consonance, and figure 32, the only example in which the interval of the eleventh appears (illustrating the use of the sixth composite form of the diapente in organum).

73. 128.214–5 (*cum praefatis natura nostra partibus compacta constet*). This is the Boethian notion of *musica humana*. Cf. Boethius, *De inst. mus.* 1.2 (Friedlein 188.26–189.5).

74. 128.222f. (*sive sint principales, quorum est unitas differentia*). This is taken directly from Boethius, *De inst. mus.* 3.1 (Friedlein 269.2).

number 12 increase it to make 18. Let the sesquitertian to the number 18 increase it to make 24. And thus the number 24, the double of the number 12, is completed by the sesquialter and the sesquitertian.

Alternately, [130] let the sesquitertian to the number 6 increase it to 8. Let the sesquialter to the sesquitertian increase it to 12. Accordingly, the number 12, the duple of the number 6, is completed by the sesquitertian and the sesquialter. Likewise, let the sesquitertian to the number 12 increase it to 16. Let the sesquialter to the sesquitertian [that is, 16] increase it to 24. And so 24, the duple of 12, is completed by means of the sesquitertian and the sesquialter. Thus, a duple is always completed by expansion through the sesquialter and sesquitertian. In turn, the sesquialter and sesquitertian are connected by the common measure of the epogdous [9:8], so that if you take away the epogdous from the sesquialter you make a sesquitertian; when it [the epogdous] in turn is added to the sesquitertian, it reestablishes the sescuple [=sesquialter]. Therefore, it is established that tones coming together in agreement take their concord from numbers coming together in agreement.

D. This has been clearly explained.

M. Pay attention to how the [tones] sounding agreeably together are not in [just] any combinations. But as, for example, the number 24 is the duple of 12, the triple of 8, the quadruple of 6, the sesquialter of 16, the epitritus of 18, the subduple of 48, the subepitritus of 32, [and] the subsescuple of 36, so indeed any phthongus sounds with another [phthongus] a diapason, with another a diapason-plus-diapente, with another a disdiapason, with another a diapente, with another a diatessaron, with another a subdiapason, with another a subdiatessaron, [and] with another a subdiapente; and this would not happen except that they are related by their commensurality on the basis of multiple and superparticular relationships. [131]

How it may be known by what proportion any symphony is formed

D. Although it has been sufficiently shown that the principle of commensurality joins musical pitches to one another, how nevertheless can one know to which proportion any symphony must be assigned? For how is it known that the diapason must be assigned to the duple relationship, the diapente to the sescuple, the diatessaron to the epitritus, the diapente-plus-diapason to the triple, [and] the disdiapason to the quadruple?

M. The first proof of this matter is that, just as one duple is always made up of a sesquialter and a sesquitertian in the manner described, so do two smaller symphonies, that is, the diapente and the diatessaron, make up a diapason, which contains eight steps (*voculae*), as in figure 41.[75] For whether [you begin] from the lower or from the higher part—either you measure up to the fourth step, then

---

75. 131.*descriptio* 2. In this diagram can be seen the first synthesis of aspects of the two tonal systems, that of the *Enchiriadis* treatises and that of the Greater Perfect System of the Greek harmonics tradition.

Figure 41

to the fifth from there; or the fifth step is measured, then the fourth beyond—one symphony is always made out of two. That would not happen if other symphonies were used to complete [the diapason] or if other symphonies were being completed.

Concerning this, [132] Boethius has said:

Which of all the consonance we have mentioned ought to be thought the better one must be judged both by the ear and by reason. For in the way the ear is affected by tones and the eye by visible form, so the judgment of reason is affected by number or by continuous quantity. Thus, given a number or line, nothing is easier to recognize with the eye or reason than its double,[76]

as, for example, 12 to 6.

Likewise, after the judgment of the duple follows that of the half or subduple; after the half, that of the triple; after the triple that of the third part. And because the recognition of the duple is easier,[77]

it is justly assigned to that consonance which is easier and which our critical faculty[78] perceives more clearly.

Therefore, the first and sweetest[79] consonance is made at the eighth step and is called the diapason [as 12:6]. After the duple [here, 12] is that which exceeds [the base number and subduple 6] by half of the subduple [½ × 6 = 3], that is, the sescuple [9], as 9:6; and that which exceeds [the sescuple] by twice its size, that is, the triple, such as 18:6. Therefore, since these two proportions, although in a contrary arrangement, follow next after the duple, these symphonies can be ascribed properly to those which we perceive by ear to be the next in rank after the diapason, that is, the diapente and the diapason-plus-diapente. Since tones that span a diatessaron are the least consonant, [133] we aptly assign this con-

76. 132.286–91. Quoted from Boethius, *De inst. mus.* 1.32 (Friedlein 222.14–20).

77. 132.291–3. Quoted from Boethius, *De inst. mus.* 1.32 (Friedlein 222.20–2).

78. 132.294 (*sensus*). I adopt here Calvin Bower's translation of this word, which, as he points out, cannot refer to the senses, regarded as untrustworthy by the Pythagoreans. Cf. Boethius, *Fundamentals of Music,* p. 73 n. 47.

79. 132.295 (*prima suavisque consonantia*). This phrase is found at Boethius, *De inst. mus.* 2.18 (Friedlein 249.23). It introduces a passage (continuing through the direct quote at 133.308f.) that paraphrases materials on the ranking of consonances in Boethius, *De inst. mus.* 1.32 (Friedlein 222.13–27) and 2.19 (Friedlein 250.26–251.14). This order is different from that previously given in SE at 124.146ff.; neither listing, however, includes the eleventh.

cord to that proportion wherein the larger number exceeds the lesser by a third part of the lesser; this is the epitritus, as 8 to 6. Because the tones that sound the concord of the disdiapason are the farthest apart, we justly ascribe [them] to that proportion which separates [the terms] by a four-fold amount, as 24 to 6.[80] In such succession is fixed the extent (*modus*) of the concords, which can be neither extended beyond the quadruple [4:1] nor compressed under the third part [4:3].[81] So the consonances have assumed this ranking, in which the large ones (*augmenta*) are expressed in numbers of multiple relationship [and the] compact ones (*detrimenta*) in exactly the opposite way, in numbers of superparticular relationship.[82]

Another argument with convincing evidence, which adds credence to the explanation given above not only audibly but visually, is also given [here]. Strings or pipes,[63] if they are of equal width and if the length of the greater is twice the smaller, will sound together the diapason, as has been said above. If [the larger] contains [the smaller] three times they will answer at the diapason-plus-diapente. If four times, they make the concord of the disdiapason. If the larger half is half again as large as the smaller, the consonance will be a diapente. If it is greater by a third part of the smaller, it will be a diatessaron. If it is larger by an eighth part of the smaller, they will sound together a whole tone. [134]

Why not more than three species of the multiple [ratio] pertain to music, and why there are no more than three species of superparticular

D. It has now been clearly proven through detailed demonstration not only that music is produced from connumerate or commensurate numbers, but also which symphonies are bound to these species of connumerate numbers. I wonder, however,

---

80. 133.305–7 (*Quia maxime . . . XXIIII contra VI*). This expresses in different words the content of Boethius, *De inst. mus.* 2.18 (Friedlein 250.17f.).

81. 133.308–9 (*Ac stat deinceps . . . coartari*). This is a direct quotation from Boethius, *De inst. mus.* 2.18 (Friedlein 250.20–2). However, the present context alters the original meaning, for the order of the concords given in Boethius—that of the Pythagoreans, according to Nicomachus—is given as diapason, diapason-plus-diapente, bisdiapason, diapente, and diatessaron, whereas in SE the consonances have been derived in the order diapason, diapente, diapason-plus-diapente, diatessaron, and bisdiapason.

82. 133.309–11 (*Sicque hunc ordinem . . . detrimenta*). This neutral statement about the basis of the consonances is taken almost verbatim from Boethius, *De inst. mus.* 2.18 (Friedlein 249.29–250.1). However, there the subject of the sentence (*reliquae*) refers to consonances other than the diapason.

83. 133.314 (*Fidiculae sive fistulae*). Boethius refers frequently to strings as *chordae* but never as *fidiculae;* moreover, he never discusses pipe measurements, which were to have important applications from the Carolingian period onward, as organs began to appear in the West. The passage beginning here is the first of several practical, didactic demonstrations that follow the exposition of various aspects of harmonic theory. The classic study of medieval tracts dealing with pipe measurements is Klaus-Jürgen Sachs, *Mensura fistularum: Die Mensurierung der Orgelpfeifen im Mittelalter*, vol. 1 (Stuttgart: Musikwissenschaftliche Verlag-Gesellschaft, 1970). See also Phillips *Sources*, pp. 155f.

why only three forms of multiple [ratio] and only three forms of superparticular are alloted to music, [and] why only the duple, triple, and quadruple relationships [and] only the sesquialter and the sesquitertian with sesquioctave measure out (*modulari*) consonances.

M. There is nothing larger than the bisdiapason, that is, larger than the quadruple [relationship], for this reason: because nature assigns this characteristic (*modus*) to tones, namely that when the individual consonances in the disdiapason are distributed through the individual steps (*discrimina*) of the seven pitches within a diapason,[84] the duple symphonies cannot proceed further. On the other hand, the intervals cannot be reduced to less than a third part, that is, below an epitritus, because a third part is less than a half, a fourth less than a third, a fifth less than a fourth, a sixth less than a fifth part, and so on. Whereas the sesquialter, which is the interval of the half [such as 3:2], contains three whole tones plus a semitone, and the epitritus, which is the interval of the third part [such as 4:3], holds two whole tones plus a semitone, [135] it happens that the smaller intervals can neither contain two whole tones plus a semitone nor be commensurable if they are of two whole tones or of one and a half. Only the sesquioctave interval, because its size encompasses a whole-tone, is allowed.

D. Why does the compass of a whole tone fall only in this proportion?

M. Because this proportion alone is generated by the ratio between the sesquialter and sesquitertian.

D. How is it born out of the sesquialter and sesquitertian when they are subtracted?[85]

M. Is it not easily understood that, for example, the number 6 increases by half to its sesquialter, that is, the number 9? And by a third part to its epitritus, that is, the number 8? But just as the number 9 is the sesquialter to the number 6, so is it the sesquioctave to the epitritus [8]. Likewise, half of 12 is evenly contained in its sesquialter 18, [and] a third [of 12] is evenly contained in its epitritus 16. But just as the number 18 is the sesquialter to 12, so it makes the sesquioctave to the epitritus [16].

D. I understand.

M. For this reason, take note at the same time that an interval between two [consecutive] tones can be neither greater nor less than an integral whole tone, that is, as much as the difference first measured between the sesquialter and sesquitertian [ratios].[86] Therefore, with sesquialter and sesquitertian [ratios]—whose

84. 134.331–2 (*septenarum . . . vocum discrimina*). This wording recalls the frequently used citation from Vergil that is also found in ME at 33.27f.: *obloquitur numeris septem discrimina vocum.*

85. 135.344 (*ex comparatis*). The comparison of two intervals involves "subtracting" them to obtain the difference; this is done mathematically by dividing their ratios. Hence, here 3/2 divided by 4/3 = 9/8.

86. 135.352–5. The whole tone, not the semitone, is considered the smallest distance between two consecutive tones. This is explained by the assertion that the whole tone is the smallest interval said to be commensurate and hence suitable for music. The semitone, which in the *Enchiriadis* treatises is critically important for the determination of mode and accurate

intervals, of course, are completed commensurally [136] by whole tones plus semitones, as has been said—there is commensurality only through sesquioctave intervals. In turn, only sesquialter and sesquitertian intervals are commensurate with duples and quadruples, whose intervals are similarly filled in by them. For the sesquiquartal and sesquiquintal and the remaining smaller intervals there is no commensuration whatever—not with the duple, nor with the triple, nor with the quadruple, nor with the sescuple—and on that account they are excluded from music.

Now I should also like to confirm the kindred commensurality of strings and pipes by means of the [common] measures in the above proportions that are admitted to music. You take two strings or pipes, the larger being in sescuple [proportion to the smaller, such as 9:6]. You take the epitritus of the sescuple and thus you have made the duple [$\frac{4}{3} \times 9 = 12$]. Now that which is the epitritus to the second[87] is twice as long as the first [$\frac{4}{3} \times 9 = 12$]. Conversely you measure out the epitritus, string to string or pipe to pipe [$\frac{4}{3} \times 6 = 8$]; you take the sesquialter of the epitritus; and the duple is made [$\frac{3}{2} \times 8 = 12$]. Put these in order, as 6, 8, 9, 12, and you will discover a properly measured epogdous between the two middle [strings or pipes]; that is, the longer string or pipe is greater by an eighth part of the smaller.

Likewise in another way: [137] measure out two pipes, the longer in duple [proportion, 12:6]. For the short pipe you measure out the epitritus [$6 \times \frac{4}{3} = 8$]. For the long pipe you measure out the subepitritus [$12 \times \frac{3}{4} = 9$]. And you place in order the subduple, epitritus, subepitritus, [and] duple [6, 8, 9, 12], and thus the epogdous falls naturally between the two middle terms. From this interval [the epogdous] a sescuple is made to its farther side, on the one hand, [and] the epitritus [is made] to its nearer side on the other. Further, if you double the epitritus, the sescuple, and the duple [8, 9, 12], you have made simultaneously another diapason [12, 16, 18, 24] of the same arrangement as before [figure 42].

D. In what way do the other superparticular relationships [138] not have commensurality with the duple and quadruple ones?

M. So that this will be clear to you, let me begin to illustrate from the number 12, the smallest number possible here. For the whole quantity of this number is contained evenly in 24, half of it in 18, a third of it in 16, [and] a fourth of it in 15. But the number 18, which is the sesquialter to 12, is made commensural to 24 by the epitritus ratio. Moreover, the number 16, which is the epitritus to 12, is made commensurate to 24 by the sescuple ratio. However, the number 15, which is the

---

singing, presents awkward problems from the point of harmonic theory, burdened as it is by its ungainly ratio (256:243). The ambiguous role of the semitone is suggested at 124f.155–61, where the semitone—which is not described in terms of a ratio like the other intervals—is added to the diapason, diapason-plus-diapente, disdiapason, diapente, diatessaron, and whole tone as an interval by which "harmonic sweetness is governed."

87. 136.368 (*ad secundam*). The author seems to be thinking of the terms in ascending numerical order as they are added to the series. At this point there are only two terms, 6 and 9. Thus *ad secundam* refers to 9.

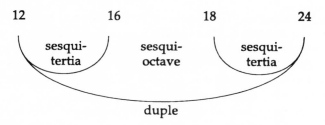

Figure 42

sesquiquartal to 12, is not commensurate with 24 but [is] dissonant because of its supertripartient form. Likewise, the number 24 is contained evenly in 48, half of it in the number 36, a third of it in the number 32, [and] a fourth of it in the number 30. But the number 36, which is the sescuple to 24, is made commensural to 48 by the epitritus ratio. Moreover, the number 32, which is the epitritus to 24, is made commensurate to 48 by the sescuple ratio. But the number 30, which is the sesquiquartal to 24, cannot be commensural with 48. You see, [139] therefore, that as soon as intervals begin to be made smaller than the sesquitertian, the superparticular [ratios] have no connumeration with the duple and for this reason [lack] any consonant combination.

D. For what reason does it happen that, in the series of tones, the epitriti are pitches a fourth apart, the sesquialter a fifth apart, the duple an octave apart, and others at their respective distances?

M. Since it is established that the duple interval is filled either by the epitritus and sesquialter or by two epitriti with an epogdous in the middle, these same intervals of the epitriti are, in turn, filled in with epogdoi. Indeed, the two middle tones in the interval of the diapason, that is, the fourth and fifth tones, sound respectively the diatessaron on one side and the diapente on the other, and each [tone of the epogdous] is distant from its respective side by an epitritus. The epogdoi, in turn, fill in the epitritus on each side according to this principle: an epitritus is divided into four tones and three intervals, so that two of the individual intervals hold single epogdoi or whole tones but the third is filled in with a limma, which is the semitone. Thus it happens that pitches of the sesquitertian are found a fourth apart and those of the sesquialter a fifth apart, whereas those of the duple are assigned an octave apart, those of the bisduple occupy places a fifteenth apart, and those of the triple a twelfth.

D. I ask, according to what principle or in what order in the series of tones are the whole tones joined with semitones?

M. You will be able to perceive that more clearly if I explain first what the arithmetic, geometric, and harmonic means are.

D. Explain, I beg you.

M. After proportions, proportionalities are considered. For a proportion is a relationship of two terms (termini), whereas proportionality [140] involves no fewer than three. Therefore, proportionality is formed through either an arithmetic, a geometric, or a harmonic mean. We call a mean that where, by a joining of one or two limits (*limites*), two extremities are bound into a concord. We call the numerical amounts (*summae numerorum*) the limits or terms [of a proportion]. The *arithmetic mean,* then, is that which is equidistant to the terms, but these terms are not in the same ratio to the mean, as you perceive in 1, 2, 3.[88]

D. I perceive, indeed, that 1 to 2 is the duple and 2 to 3 the sesquialter.

M. The *geometric mean* is that in which not the differences [between pairs of terms] but the proportions are considered equal, as you see in 1, 2, 4.

D. I do indeed see this, because just as 2 is the duple of 1, so is 4 that of 2.

M. The *harmonic mean* is that in which neither the same proportions nor the same differences are sought; rather, the outside terms are to each other as are the differences between [the middle and each of the outside] terms, as you observe [in] 3, 4, 6.

D. I see that the outside terms as also the differences between the [middle and each of the outside] terms differ by double.[89]

M. Therefore, it has been necessary to see first by which mean the distances between tones are determined. The individual means are appropriate for different things; music, however, is seen to be put together from all of these. The geometric mean joins all terms of the duples to one another, so that 12 is to 6 as 24 is to 12, and 24 is to 12 [141] as 48 is to 24. Then these intervals of the duples are filled in with two terms, one of these joining two extremes together through the arithmetic, the other through the harmonic, mean. Thus, by whatever the number 9 exceeds 6, it is exceeded by 12; and by whatever number 18 exceeds 12, it is exceeded by 24—precisely by the arithmetic mean. In turn, by whatever fraction 8 exceeds 6, 12 exceeds 8 by this same fraction of itself. For you understand that the number 8 is larger than the number 6 by [the latter's] third part, and the number 12 is larger than 8 by a third part of [the former]. Likewise, 12 is related to 16 and 16 in turn to 24 through the harmonic mean.

D. I see also that it happens that the differences are in that proportion by which the extreme terms are related to each other: that, by whatever fraction of the number 6 [the number] 8 differs, 12 differs from 8 by this same fraction. For just as 6 is to 12, so 2 is to 4: between 6 and 8 the difference is 2, between 8 and 12 it is 4.

M. You certainly understand correctly. Now hear how the whole tones that fill the intervals of the terms mentioned above are neither mutually diminished and increased by equal parts, as diesis to diesis,[90] through the arithmetic mean, nor are

---

88. 140.427ff. SE's definitions of the three means succinctly paraphrase Boethius, *De inst. mus.* 2.12 (Friedlein 241.14–242.12). Algebraically expressed, the arithmetic, geometric and harmonic means of the terms x and y are $(x + y)/2$, $\sqrt{xy}$, and $2xy/(x + y)$, respectively.

89. That is, of the outside terms, 6 is twice 3; of the differences of the three terms, the difference between 6 and 4 is twice that between 2 and 1.

90. 141.456–8 (*ipsi toni . . . dies ad dies*). This is the only use in SE of the Greek term διεσις (Lat. *diesis*), here in a novel abbreviated Latinized form, although *diesis* appears in ME at 21.17. That whole tones are not equally divisible into equal parts and that the "semitone" as "diesis" (256/243) is really less than half a whole tone are demonstrated in Boethius, *De inst. mus.*

they of dissimilar proportions according to the harmonic mean. [142] Rather, the epitritus and sesquialter intervals are filled in when the geometric mean is measured out. For just as the second [term] is a sesquioctave to the first, so is the third to the second. Just as the number 72 is the sesquioctave to 64, so is the number 81 the sesquioctave to 72.

D. I now understand how one whole tone after another is measured by means of these numbers. But tell, why do you choose these numbers for the sake of example?

M. Because this cannot be demonstrated by a number smaller than the number 8 times 8, which is 64. Because this last number is an octuple, it produces two sesquioctaves out of itself. For an eighth of the number 64 added to the same number produces the number 72; furthermore, an eighth part of the number 72 added to the same number produces 81, and thus two sesquioctaves are made: 64, 72, 81. Since it has been proposed to explain more fully both how, in the epitritus interval, two whole tones are disposed with a semitone, and also how, in the entire series of steps,[91] semitones are disposed with whole tones, a fourth term ought to be designated which is the epitritus to the first, between which and the third term the semitone is placed. But since the number 64 cannot be divided into three equal [parts], the epitritus is not added to it. Therefore it is multiplied by 3 and then the epitritus is added to it. Therefore 64 times 3 produces what number?

D. 192.

M. Yes; [and] from this number we take the starting point for explaining these things which we have undertaken. Give me its double.

D. Twice 192 makes 384. [143]

M. Indeed. See, you have these two numbers in a duple interval: 192, 384. Now it is necessary that we fill in this duple interval with two epitriti. Therefore, give the epitritus of the number 192.

D. A third part of the number 192, that is, 64, added to the same number produces 256. Since this number is an epitritus to the subduple term [that is, 192], the sesquialter to the duple arises.

M. Give the sescuple of the same number 192.

D. A half part of the number 192, that is, 96, added to it makes 288. Since this number is a sescuple to a subduple term, the epitritus to the duple arises.

M. So it is, indeed. Now let these four terms be arranged in order: 192, 256, 288, 384. Since there is an epitritus interval between the first and second terms, [and] likewise an epitritus interval between the third and fourth terms, let us fill in these intervals of the epitriti with whole tones and semitones. I take an eighth part of the number 192, which is 24; the number 216, the second step, is made through

---

2.28f. (Friedlein 260.20–263.19); that SE's author knows this becomes clear at 146.525–9. But what SE's author is trying to say here is that, represented numerically, successive boundaries of whole tones are not the same distance apart, although proportionally the same, as in the series 64, 72, 81, where 72/64 and 81/72 are both 9:8 ratios.

91. 142.472 (*sonorum serie*). For clarity, from this point on, *sonus* and *locus* will be translated as "step" wherever referring to degrees of the scale being constructed.

the addition of the whole tone. I take the eighth part of the number 216, which is 27, and the number 243, the third step, is made by this addition of a whole tone. I cannot take the eighth part of the number 243, because between this and the fourth term, 256, which is the epitritus to the first [⁴⁄₃ × 192], there [144] are found exactly thirteen units, which is the amount in the ratio of the semitone [256/243]. Thus, the measured-out structure (*modulatio*) of the diatessaron is completed, calculated from two whole tones and a semitone.

Since, in turn, the sescuple is greater [than the epitritus] by the ratio of an epogdous, I take from the fourth step, 256, its eighth part, which is 32; the number 288, the fifth step, is thus produced through the addition of this whole tone. Then from the fifth step [the number 288] I take an eighth part, which is 36, and the number 324, the sixth step, is made through the addition of this whole tone. From the sixth step I take away its eighth part, which is 40½, and the number 364½, the seventh step, is made through the addition of this whole-tone. However, from the seventh step to the number 384, which is the eighth step, 19½ units remain as the amount in the ratio of the semitone. Thus, the measured-out structure of the diapente is completed, calculated from three whole tones and a semitone. [145] [Here is] an illustration of this [figure 43].

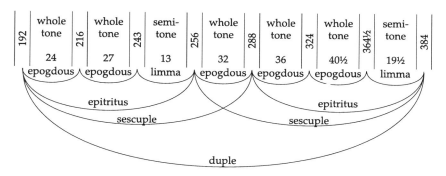

Figure 43

If you also desire proof of the measurements, you make a string or pipe greater than another string or pipe by an epitritus, which must be placed at the fourth step. Also you make [another one] longer by a sesqualter, which is located at the fifth step. You make [another one] longer by double, which you put at the eighth step. Likewise, taking the eighth part of the first string or pipe, you calculate the [position of] the second [string or pipe]; taking an eighth part of the second [146] you calculate the third.

You will not be able to take an eighth [part] of the third for measuring out the fourth, which now takes [its] measure from the first, relative to which an epitritus is made. Likewise, again it is not necessary that the fifth be measured by means of the fourth, because, although it is the sescuple of the first, it is made out of the sesquioctave of the epitritus. Again, you measure the sixth, taking an eighth part of the fifth. You measure the seventh, taking an eighth part of the sixth. [But] you will not be able to measure the eighth by means of the seventh, because, since the epitritus is made by the eighth against the fifth, the distance between the seventh and the eighth will be a semitone. By this disposition of the intervals the different pitches come together in sweet conjunction.

D. It is certainly to be marvelled at that the pitches are not otherwise able to make concord unless the intervals of semitones are compressed—at one time within the epitritus space, at another time within the sesquialter—so that their size is less than half [that] of the preceding whole tone.[92]

M. In fact, this happens for an astonishing and divine reason. So that you may understand everything with certainty, let us also try to take up the division of the monochord by these same rules, for it is already known that the longer strings or pipes produce lower tones, and for this reason higher [tones] will be [produced] by shorter [strings or pipes], so that a half part sounds a duple, a fourth part a quadruple.

Therefore, let a string be stretched as between A and Z [in figure 44]. If I take half of this distance, as from H to Z, then the half, when struck, sounds a diapason to [147] the whole. If I take half of the half, as from H to P, then the bisdiapason [to AZ] sounds. Likewise, the smaller symphonies are disposed in both diapason spans, that is, in AH within AZ and again in HP within HZ. If I take a fourth part of the span AZ, then DZ answers [AZ] at a diatessaron. If I take the third part, then EZ answers [AZ] at a diapente. Similarly, if a fourth part of the span HP is taken away, the diatessaron [to HP] sounds, and if a third part is taken away, it will be the diapente [to HP].

Now let us divide up the spans of diatessaron and diapente with epogdoi. For truly, when a ninth part of the span AZ is removed, there will be the whole tone BZ [to AZ], [and] when the ninth part of the span BZ is taken away, there will be the whole tone CZ [to BZ] and the semitone DZ [to CZ]. Since the difference of diatessaron and diapente is a whole tone, there is also the whole tone DZ to EZ. When a ninth part of the span EZ is taken away, there will be the whole tone FZ [to EZ]. When a ninth part of the span FZ is removed, there will be the whole tone GZ [to FZ] and the semitone HZ [to GZ], and the interval of the diapason is completed. By the same manner in another diapason, that is, in the span HP within HZ, you will arrange the whole tones with semitones through the diatessaron and diapente intervals by the principles of diatonic melody[93] [figure 44[94]]. [148]

92. 146.525–8 (*Mirum certe . . . perveniant*). See note to 141.456–8.

93. 147.549 (*diatonici modulaminis*). In Boethius, *De inst. mus.* 1.22f. (Friedlein 215.20 and 216.20), "diatonic" refers to the *genus diatonicus,* defined as the division of the tetrachord into two whole tones and a semitone and contrasted with the "chromatic" and "enharmonic" genera. The standard, diatonic form of the Greater Perfect System is conventionally represented as a two-octave natural minor scale on A, but the scale that results from SE's monochord division corresponds to the modern C-major scale. (See also introduction, "Demonstrations.") Nonetheless, this new division is "diatonic" in that semitones occur only after two and three whole tones (as in the diatonic form of the Greater Perfect System), and in that there are no inter-

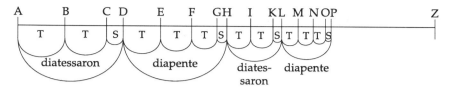

Figure 44

D. Since there are four species of tetrachord following one another, how can each one have the same disposition of whole tones and semitones?

M. By no means can they. For when there is one tetrachord that consists of two whole tones and a semitone, and the next tetrachord is made one whole tone higher, the latter will consist of whole tone, semitone, and whole tone. That which follows this tetrachord at the third step and is higher by a whole tone necessarily consists of a semitone and two whole tones. Then that which is at the fourth step follows in turn; it is one semitone away from the preceding and encompasses three whole tones. But that which is at the fifth step will again be of two whole tones and a semitone, returning to the first arrangement.

D. Are these individual dispositions [149] proper to the individual species of tetrachord?

M. They certainly are. And because the order of this disposition recurs at the fifth step, the same quality of melody returns five steps away.

D. But for what reason?

M. Whenever a semitone falls between steps, it gives the nature (*forma*) of the tritus to the higher [and] the nature of the deuterus to the lower.[95] The remaining steps, however, [receive their nature] according to how many whole tones they are from the semitone. For that tone which we call archous or protus is one whole tone away from the semitone above and two whole tones from that below. And we call tetrardus that which is two whole tones away from that above and one from that below.

   Now you can easily distinguish between tetrachords, because that which is disposed with two whole tones and a semitone in ascending order consists of the tones ⁊ tetrardus [C], ℉ protus [D], ℉ deuterus [E], and ∫ tritus [F]. That which is disposed by whole tone, semitone, and whole tone consists of the protus tone ℉

---

vals smaller than a semitone. *Modulamen,* translated here as "melody," must be understood as an abstract series of intervals measured out for purposes of theoretical demonstration.

   94. 147.*descriptio* 5 (fig. 44). The use of the unexpected scale on C that is the basis for many of the diagrams in SE, part 3 may be related to the demonstrations requiring instruments in this section. Hucbald, *De harmonica institutione (GS* 1:110b–111a, transl. Babb, pp. 24f.) also gives a scale on C, saying that it corresponds to that used by water organs and strings. The model for using the letters A–P, also used by Hucbald, is undoubtedly Boethius, *De inst. mus.* 4.17 (Friedlein 347.20).

   95. 149.562–4. This recalls the principles stated in part 1, 66.102–6.

[D], deuterus $\digamma$ [E], tritus $\int$ [F], and tetrardus $\curlyvee$ [G]. That which is disposed by a semitone and two whole tones consists of deuterus $\digamma$ [E], tritus $\int$ [F], tetrardus $\curlyvee$ [G], and protus $\int$ [a]. That which is disposed with three whole tones consists of tritus $\int$ [F], tetrardus $\curlyvee$ [G], protus $\int$ [a], and deuterus $\int$ [b]. So that it can be made clearer, let figure 45 be an illustration of the individual tetrachords. [150] In this illustration of the four tetrachords, therefore, the whole-tone distances are marked by the interspersed blank boxes, and the lines placed between the steps signal that the steps are separated by semitones. Inside the boxes is indicated the nature (*proprietas*) of each respective tone.

D. Certainly this is easily seen, but why is one tetrachord made of three whole tones?

M. This is to be understood from the things said previously. Since two tetrachords fill one diapason, and these individual tetrachords are made of two whole tones and a semitone, and since the middle integral whole tone separates the two tetrachords, it happens that the form of the fourth tetrachord is made up of three whole tones when it exceeds the space of a diatessaron, that is, two whole tones plus a semitone. That also is evident from figure 45. [151]

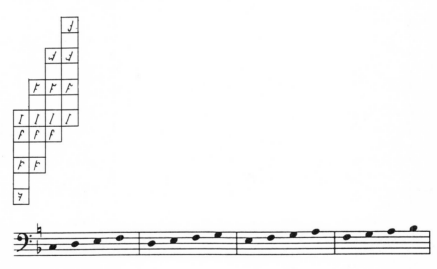

Figure 45

D. I understand this clearly now, both from the diagram and through reckoning. I see that changing the position of the semitone produces a change of the tropes.

M. Unquestionably. Hence, there is for any phthongus its discernible quality, and for tetrachords and pentachords there are their species and, as you discovered, the forms of all the tropes. Besides, somehow the semitone becomes the very heart and soul of song. Therefore, inasmuch as the nature of the semitone enables it to change the species of the phthongi, if you change the order of the semitone within two of these phthongi separated by a sesquitertian their arrangement (*forma*) will immediately be changed.

For example, make one string longer than another by an epitritus, which, of course, sounds the diatessaron between them. This consonance, since it encompasses in itself two other steps, is reckoned from the lower side, that is, from the longer string or pipe, and a whole tone is placed between the first and second [strings or pipes], likewise between the second and third. Then we separate the third from the fourth by a semitone, and the tetrachord will be disposed in these steps: tetrardus ⅂ [C], protus ᚱ [D], deuterus ᚱ [E], and tritus ∫ [F]. In turn, if [152] we were to begin from the higher side, a whole tone would separate the first and second [strings or pipes]; likewise the second and third, and there would be the amount of a semitone between the third and fourth. Then there would be another species of tetrachord, both in the position of the whole tones and in the properties of the tones. The first tone, which is the highest, then becomes protus ᚜∫ [a], the next tetrardus ᚱ [G], then tritus ∫ [F], and at the fourth step deuterus ᚱ [E], as figure 46 shows.

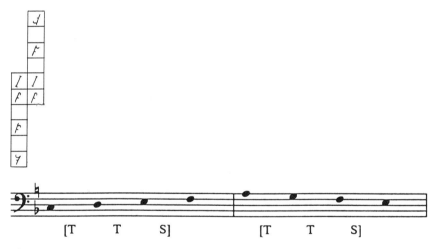

Figure 46

[153] Moreover, it must be known that only the tritus ∫ [F] and deuterus ᚱ [E] have between them the discernible quality of their properties, namely, that between these alone there is the difference of a semitone. However, for the other tones separated by a whole tone, the distinguishing property is not due to this [quality] but rather is inferred from their order [within the steps]; indeed, it can be determined easily from the context which tone one or another may be. Hence, to develop this faculty we sing the names of the phthongi in Greek,[96] rising and

96. 153.612–3 (*ipsa Greca ptongorum vocabula modulamur*) and *descriptiones* 8a–b (fig. 47a–b). This phrase and illustration parallel ME, chap. 6 (11.12f.) and the accompanying *descriptio* (fig. 6.1). SE's illustration as printed by Schmid seems to clarify how to sing the given musical phrases by using the Greek names, yet according to his critical apparatus only the tenth-

Figure 47

falling as far as a third, whereby, of course, the respective properties of the tones are discerned from their order shown [in figure 47].

D. For what reason, or in how many ways, the internal disposition of tetrachords may be varied, or how the species of modes or tropes are generated by their various individual arrangements (*positiones*)—all have been abundantly explained. However, there is still room for investigation. You said that the same category of trope (*eundem tropi modum*) returns five steps away because the same form of tetrachord (*ordo positionis*) returns.

M. I have said plainly both that, on account of the sesquialter relationship, the symphony at the fifth sounds harmoniously, and that a trope of the same category (*eiusdem modi tropum*) recurs on account of the recurring disposition of the same form [of tetrachord]. For this reason, if [the trope] is reckoned from a different step, either it will disagree with what [155] precedes, since, if it retains the quality of the trope, it will not find its proper tetrachordal form; or, yielding to another arrangement of tetrachord, it changes by transposition the trope's quality. But make known what you propose for investigation.

D. Since the category of the same trope (*eiusdem tropi modus*) is not perceived as different in a melodic series of whole tones with semitones when the arrangement is the same [at a different level], I ask: why are pitches eight steps away in concord with the same trope, since the disposition of this same arrangement does not return eight steps away?

M. Indeed, it is true that a given disposition returns in the same arrangement of steps at the fifth and ninth more than at the octave, so that, just as the first and second [steps] are separated by a whole tone, there is a whole tone between the ninth and tenth steps; just as between the second and third, so too between the tenth and eleventh. However, just as there is a semitone between the third and fourth tones, so does one separate the eleventh and twelfth. But it must be known that, in this largest symphony, a pitch that approaches a pitch at the eighth step

___

century manuscript *H* transmits that form of the example, a fact stressed by Phillips *Sources*, p. 160 n. 56; see also her review of the edition, pp. 139f. In fact, most of the other early sources, including *A,* presumably the earliest extant source, give a form in which the Greek names are not supplied.

above or below does not follow the order of its position[97] but that to which it an-swers consonantly. For consonance is not preserved if a whole tone clashes with a semitone—or a semitone with a whole tone—directly opposite.

D. How might whole tones clash with semitones?

M. When a whole tone [156] separates some phthongi but a semitone separates those eight steps away—for example, if there is a whole tone between the first and sec-ond steps as between the eighth and ninth, and there is a whole tone between the second and third steps as between the ninth and tenth, but there is a semitone between the third and fourth steps and, on the other hand, a whole tone between the tenth and eleventh. Likewise, there is a whole tone between the fourth and fifth steps, but, on the other hand, a semitone between the eleventh and twelfth. So surely, because semitones differ from whole tones there can be no duple pro-portion or the same consonance or trope between the fourth and the eleventh steps or between the fifth and twelfth. Now, provided that there is a whole tone between the eighth and ninth steps as between the first and second, a whole tone between the ninth and tenth steps as between the second and third, and a semi-tone between the tenth and eleventh steps as between third and fourth, through the concord of the corresponding whole tones and semitones of this kind the duple proportion both preserves the symphony and retains the category of trope (*modus tropi*).

97. 155.637 (*non sequitur sui loci ordinem*). That is, the pitch an octave away will not (always) correspond to the pitch eight steps away in the daseian scale, since the intervals between steps of the daseian scale are not always identical eight steps away.

Select Bibliography

[Anonymous]. *Music Handbook* [= *Musica enchiriadis*]. Translated by Leonie Rosenstiel. Colorado Springs: Colorado College Music Press, 1976.

Atkinson, Charles. " 'Harmonia' and the 'Modi, quos abusive tonos dicimus.' " In *Atti del XIV Congresso della Società Internazionale di Musicologia* [Bologna, 1987], pp. 485–500. Turin: EDT, 1990.

———. "Parapter." In *Handwörterbuch der musikalischen Terminologie* (1978), ed. Hans Heinrich Eggebrecht. Wiesbaden: Franz Steiner, 1978.

Augustine, Aurelius. *De musica.* Edited by Giovanni Marzi. Florence: G. C. Sansoni, 1969.

———. *Divine Providence and the Problem of Evil.* Edition and translation of St. Augustine's *De ordine* with annotations by Robert R. Russell. New York: Cosmpolitan Science and Art Service, 1942.

Aurelian of Réome. *Aurelian of Réome: "The Discipline of Music."* Translated by Joseph Ponte. Colorado Springs: Colorado College Music Press, 1968.

———. *Musica disciplina.* Edited by Lawrence Gushee. Corpus scriptorum de musica, vol. 21. Rome: American Institute of Musicology, 1975.

Bailey, Terence. *Commemoratio brevis de tonis et psalmis modulandis.* Ottawa: University of Ottawa Press, 1979.

———. *The Intonation Formulas of Western Chant.* Toronto: Pontifical Institute of Medieval Studies, 1974.

Barker, Andrew, ed. *Greek Musical Writings.* 2 vols. Cambridge: Cambridge University Press, 1984–9.

Bielitz, Mathias. *Musik und Grammatik.* Munich and Salzburg: Emil Katzbichler, 1977.

Blumröder, Christoph von. "Modulatio/Modulation." In *Handwörterbuch der musikalischen Terminologie,* ed. Hans Heinrich Eggebrecht. Wiesbaden: Franz Steiner, 1983.

Boethius, Anicius Manlius Severinus. *The Consolation of Philosophy.* Translated by S. J. Tester. With *The Theological Tractates.* Translated by H. F. Stewart, E. K. Rand, and S. J. Tester. Cambridge, Mass.: Harvard University Press, 1973.

————. *De institutione arithmetica libri duo. De institutione musica libri quinque. Accedit geometria quae fertur Boetii.* Edited by Gottfried Friedlein. Leipzig, 1857. Repr. Frankfurt a. M.: Minerva, 1966.

————. *De institutione musica.* Translated with introduction and notes by Calvin M. Bower as *Fundamentals of Music.* Edited by Claude V. Palisca. New Haven and London: Yale University Press, 1989.

Browning, Robert. *Medieval and Modern Greek.* 2d ed. Cambridge: Cambridge University Press, 1983.

Burney, Charles. *A General History of Music.* 3 vols. London, 1776–89. Repr. New York: Dover, 1957.

[Calcidius]. *Timaeus a Calcidio translatus commentarioque instructus.* Edited by Jan Hendrick Waszink. London: Warburg Institute, Leiden: and E. J. Brill, 1962.

Cassidorus. *Institutiones.* Edited by R. A. B. Mynors. Oxford: Clarendon Press, 1937.

Censorinus. *De die natali.* Edited by Friedrich Hultsch. Leipzig, 1867.

————. *De die natali liber.* Edited by Nicolaus Sallmann. Leipzig: Teubner, 1983.

————. *De die natali ("The Natal Day").* Translated by W. Maude. New York: Cambridge Encyclopedia Company, 1900.

Chailley, Jacques. *Alia musica.* Paris: Institut de Musicologie de l'Université de Paris, 1964.

Coussemaker, Edmond de. *Histoire de l'harmonie au Moyen Âge.* Paris: Didron, 1852.

————. *Hucbald, moine de St. Amand, et ses traits de musique.* Douai, 1841.

————. *Mémoire sur Hucbald et sur ses traits de musique.* Paris: J. Techener, 1841.

Dronke, Peter. "The Beginnings of the Sequence." *Beiträge der deutschen Sprache und Literatur* 87 (Tübingen, 1965): 43–73.

————. "Types of Poetic Art in Tropes." *Münchener Beiträge zur Mediavistik und Renaissance-Forschung* 36 (1985): 1–23.

Duchez, Marie-Elisabeth. "Jean Scot Erigène premier lecteur du *De institutione musica* de Boèce?" In *Eriugena: Studien zu seinen Quellen,* edited by Werner Beierwaltes, pp. 165–87. Heidelberg: Carl Winter, 1980.

Erickson, Raymond. "Boethius, Eriugena, and the Neoplatonism of *Musica* and *Scolica Enchiriadis.*" In *Musical Humanism and Its Legacy: Essays in Honor of Claude V. Palisca,* edited by Nancy K. Baker and Barbara R. Hanning, pp. 53–78. New York: Pendragon Press, 1992.

Forkel, Johann Nikolaus. *Allgemeine Geschichte der Musik.* 3 vols. Leipzig, 1788–1801. Repr. Graz: Akademische Druck- und Verlagsanstalt, 1967.

Fulgentius, Fabius Planciades. *Opera.* Edited by Rudolf Helm. Stuttgart: Teubner, 1970.

Gerbert, Martin, ed. *Scriptores ecclesiastici de musica sacra potissimum.* 3 vols. San-Blasius, 1784. Repr. Milan: Bollettino Bibliografico Musicale, 1931.

Guido of Arezzo. *Micrologus.* Edited by Joseph Smits van Waesberghe. [Nijmegen: American Institute of Musicology, 1955.

————. *Micrologus.* Translated by Warren Babb in *Hucbald, Guido, and John on Music.* Edited with introductions by Claude V. Palisca. New Haven and London: Yale University Press, 1978.

Gushee, Lawrence. "Questions of Genre in Medieval Treatises on Music." *Gattungen der Musik,* edited by Wulf Arlt et al., pp. 365–433. Bern and Munich: Francke, 1975.

Handschin, Jacques. "Die Musikanschauung des Johannes Scotus." *Vierteljahrsschrift für Literaturwissenschaft und Geisteswissenschaft* 5 (1927): 316–41.

Hermanus Contractus. *Musica.* Translated by Leonard Ellinwood. Rochester: Eastman School of Music, 1936.

Holladay, Richard L. "The *Musica enchiriadis* and *Scholia enchiriadis:* A Translation and Commentary." Ph.D. dissertation, The Ohio State University, 1977.

Hucbald of St. Amand. *De harmonica institutione.* Translated by Warren Babb in *Hucbald, Guido, and John on Music.* Edited, with introductions, by Claude V. Palisca. New Haven and London: Yale University Press, 1978.

Illmer, Detlef. *Formen der Erziehung und Wissensvermittlung im frühen Mittelalter.* Munich: Arbeo-Gesellschaft, 1971.

Isidore of Seville. *Etymologiarum sive originum libri XX.* Edited by W. M. Lindsay. Oxford: Clarendon Press, 1911; repr. 1962.

Jacobsthal, Gustav. *Die chromatische Alteration im liturgischen Gesang der abendländischen Kirche.* Berlin: J. Springer, 1897. Reprint, Hildesheim and New York: G. Olms, 1970.

Johannes Scottus (Eriugena). *Periphyseon (De divisione naturae), liber primus.* Edited and translated by I. P. Sheldon-Williams with Ludwig Bieler. Dublin: Dublin Institute for Advanced Studies, 1968.

————. *Eriugena: Periphyseon (The Division of Nature).* Translated by I. P. Sheldon-Williams and revised by John J. O'Meara. Montréal: Bellarmin and Washington: Dumbarton Oaks, 1987.

Keil, Heinrich, ed. *Grammatici latini ex recensione Henrici Keilii.* 7 vols. Leipzig: Teubner, 1855–80.

Laistner, M. L. W. "Notes on Greek From the Lectures of a Ninth-Century Monastery Teacher." *Bulletin of the John Rylands Library* 7 (1923):421–56.

Lausberg, Heinrich. *Handbuch der literarischen Rhetorik.* 2 vols. Munich: Max Hueber, 1970.

Lochner, Fabian. "Un manuscrit de théorie musicale provenant d'Echternach: Luxembourg, B.N. MS I:21." *Scriptorium* 42 (1988):256–61.

Maas, Martha, and Jane McIntosh Snyder. *Stringed Instruments of Ancient Greece.* New Haven and London: Yale University Press, 1989.

Macrobius, Ambrosius Theodosius. *Commentarius in Somnium Scipionis.* Edited by James A. Willis. Leipzig: Teubner, 1963.

Migne, Jacques-Paul, ed. *Patrologiae cursus completus, series latina.* Paris: Brepols, 1844–86.

Müller, Hans. *Hucbalds echte und unechte Schriften über Musik.* Leipzig, 1884.

Nicomachus of Geresa. *Introduction to Arithmetic.* Translated by Martin Luther D'Ooge. New York: Macmillan, 1926.

Oesch, Hans. *Berno und Hermann von Reichenau als Musiktheoretiker.* Bern: P. Haupt, 1961.

Phillips, Nancy. "Classical and Late Latin Sources for Ninth-Century Treatises on Music." In *Music Theory and Its Sources: Antiquity and the Middle Ages,* edited by André Barbera, pp. 100–35. Notre Dame, Ind.: University of Notre Dame Press, 1990.

————. "The Dasia Notation and Its Manuscript Tradition." In *Musicologie médiévale: Notations et séquences,* edited by Michel Huglo, pp. 157–73. Paris: Libraire Honoré Champion, 1987.

————. "*Musica* and *Scolica Enchiriadis:* The Literary, Theoretical, and Musical Sources." Ph.D. dissertation, New York University, 1984.

————. Review of Hans Schmid, ed., *Musica et scolica enchiriadis una cum aliquibus tractatulis adiunctis. Journal of the American Musicological Society* 36 (1983):129–43.

Phillips, Nancy, and Michel Huglo. "The Versus *Rex caeli:* Another Look at the So-Called Archaic Sequence." *Journal of the Plainsong and Medieval Music Society* 5 (1982):36–43.

Ptolemy, Claudius. *Ptolemaios und Porphyrios über die Musik.* Ed. Ingemar Düring. Göteborg: Elanders boktr., 1934. Reprint, Hildesheim and New York: G. Olms, 1987.

Raasted, Jorgen. "Papadike." *The New Grove Dictionary of Music and Musicians,* ed. Stanley Sadie, 14:166f. London: Macmillan, 1980.

Reckow, Fritz. "Organum." In *Handwörterbuch der musikalischen Terminologie,* ed. Hans Heinrich Eggebrecht. Wiesbaden: Franz Steiner, 1972.

————. "Organum-Begriff und frühe Mehrstimmigkeit." *Forum musicologica* 1 (Bern: Francke, 1975):31–167.

Sachs, Klaus-Jürgen. *Mensura fistularum: Die Mensurierung der Orgelpfeifen im Mittelalter.* Vol. 1. Stuttgart: Musikwissenschaftliche Verlag-Gesellschaft, 1970.

Schlecht, Raymund. "Die *Musica enchiriadis* von Hucbald." *Monatshefte für Musikgeschichte* 6–8 (1874–6):163–91, 1–93 and 89–101.

Schmid, Hans, ed. *Musica et scolica enchiriadis una cum aliquibus tractatulis adiunctis.* Munich: Verlag der Bayerischen Akademie der Wissenschaften, 1981.

————. "Zur sogenannten Pariser Bearbeitung du Musica Enchiriadis." In *Tradition und wertung: Festschrift für Franz Brunhölzl zum 65. Geburtstag,* pp. 211–8. Singnaringen: Jan Thorbecke, 1989.

Sowa, Heinrich. "Textvariationen zur Musica Enchiriadis." *Zeitschrift für Musikwissenschaft* 17 (1935):194–207.

Spitta, Phillip. "Die *Musica enchiriadis* und ihr Zeitalter." *Vierteljahrsschrift für Musikwissenschaft* 5 (1889):443–82.

Steglich, Rudolf. *Die Quaestiones in musica.* Leipzig: Breitkopf und Härtel, 1911.

Strunk, Oliver. *Essays on Music in the Byzantine World.* New York: Norton, 1977.

————. "The Tonal System of Byzantine Music." *Musical Quarterly* 28 (1942):190–204.

Thesaurus linguae latinae. Leipzig: Teubner, 1900–.

Treitler, Leo. "Reading and Singing: On the Genesis of Occidental Music-Writing." *Early Music History* 4 (1984):135–208.

Vergil. *The Eclogues and Georgics of Virgil* [Latin and English]. Translated by C. Day Lewis. Garden City, N.Y.: Doubleday, 1964.

————. *Virgil's Works: The Aeneid, Eclogues, Georgics.* Translated by J. W. Mackail, with an introduction by William C. McDermott. New York: Random House, 1950.

Vitruvius. *On Architecture [De architectura].* Edited and translated by Frank Granger. 2 volumes. London: W. Heinemann, and Cambridge, Mass.: Harvard University Press, 1931–4; repr. 1962.

Waeltner, Ernst. *Die Lehre von Organum bis zur Mitte des 11. Jahrhunderts.* Tutzing: Hans Schneider, 1975.

————. *Organicum melos: Zur Musikanschauung des Iohannes Scottus (Eriugena).* Munich: Bayerische Akademie der Wissenschaften, 1977.

Waite, William G. Review of Guido of Arezzo, *Micrologus,* edited by Joseph Smits Van Waesberghe. *Journal of the American Musicological Society* 9 (1956):146–9.

Wille, Günther. *Musica romana: Die Bedeutung der Musik im Leben der Römer.* Amsterdam: Schippers, 1967.

Williams, Peter. "Organ." In *The New Grove Dictionary of Music and Musicians,* ed. Stanley Sadie, 13:710–79. London: Macmillan, 1980.

Wiora, Walter. "Das vermeintliche Zeugnis des Johannes Eriugena für die Anfänge der abendländishen Mehrstimmigkeit." *Acta musicologica* 43 (1971):33–43.

Index

This index includes technical terms found in the Latin text and the translations as well as references to ancient and late-classical authors; modern authors are indexed only where commentary on their writings occurs.